The Book of
HILSEA

Gateway to Portsmouth

JANE SMITH

HALSGROVE

First published in 2002 by Halsgrove
Copyright © 2002 Jane Smith

All rights reserved. No part of this publication may be reproduced, stored in a retrieval system, or transmitted in any form or by any means, electronic, photocopying, recording or otherwise, without the prior permission of the copyright holder.

ISBN 1 84114 131 3

British Library Cataloguing-in-Publication Data
A CIP record for this title is available from the British Library

HALSGROVE
Halsgrove House
Lower Moor Way
Tiverton EX16 6SS
T: 01884 243242
F: 01884 243325
www.halsgrove.com

Printed and bound by
Bookcraft Ltd., Midsomer Norton

This book is dedicated to the memory of

Billy Duggan

20 February 1916 – 11 August 2001

A street party (date unknown) for the children of Horsea Road which was organised by the residents to celebrate the coronation of Queen Elizabeth II on Tuesday 2 June 1953. They provided all the food and put up the bunting in the background. The party was ceremonially opened by Dr Phillip James (*second from left*) who practised at the surgery in Copnor Road, the nearest one to Hilsea Crescent at this time.

Other local residents shown in the picture include Elsie Ward (first left) and pictured immediately below her is her grandson Anthony Craigie. The coal lorry in the background was owned by Bill Ruffell who ran the fruit shop in Hilsea Market nearby. He took the children for a ride in it while the food was being prepared.

The cake was obviously a special one for the occasion iced in red, white and blue and all the children are wearing paper coronation hats. The old type of drinking straws shown here were made of twisted waxed paper which quickly unravelled if they got too soggy.

CONTENTS

Acknowledgements		6
Introduction		7
Chapter 1	1066–1500: THE LAND RAISED IN MARSH	11
Chapter 2	1500–1900: RURAL HINTERLAND OR MILITARY FRONTIER?	13
Chapter 3	1880–1914: PORTSMOUTH'S LATE-VICTORIAN SUBURBIA	21
Chapter 4	1919–1939: A NEW LIFE AROUND HILSEA CRESCENT	29
Chapter 5	1927: THE NEW PORTSBRIDGE	33
Chapter 6	1930–1935: ART DECO HITS HILSEA	35
Chapter 7	1929–1939: HILSEA LIDO: THE PLEASURE PARK IN THE NORTH	57
Chapter 8	1939–1945: WARTIME AND THE AMERICANS	79
Chapter 9	1946–1952: LIFE RETURNS TO NORMAL	83
Chapter 10	1953–1968: A CORONATION AND A NEW LOOK TO OLD PLEASURES	99
Chapter 11	1969–1999: THE CONSTRUCTION OF THE M275 AND THE 1980s	127
Chapter 12	1990–2002: A NEW MILLENNIUM AND A GOLDEN JUBILEE	133
Bibliography		159

ACKNOWLEDGEMENTS

I have loved working on this book and have received tremendous help and support throughout from the people of Hilsea. It could not possibly have been written without the help of Ron Boyland, Bill Ferrett, and the members of the Hilsea 1940s' Club; Elsie Craigie and ladies of the Thursday Club and Mary Mullinger. Ron, Bill, Elsie and Mary also very generously lent me copies of their family photographs.

I have also had a lot of help and information from a variety of local people and I have very much enjoyed working with them all, in particular Alan Lambert who lent me photographs and read through my manuscript for me, John Bowring who lent me postcards from his specialist collection, and Eileen Cole and her family who lent me photographs and told me all about life in the prefabs.

My thanks also go to: Brian Wright, ex-RAOC, for walking me around the former Hilsea Barracks site; Maggie and Chris Ballard of the Southsea Collectors' Fair; Bob Irwin of J.A. Hewes (Photographers), 91 Lawrence Road, Southsea for his technical expertise and local knowledge; Norma Young of the Portsmouth Society for her enthusiasm, especially for Hilsea Lido; Anthea and Peter Nex for being my aunt and uncle; Nigel Pudner for permission to dedicate the book to the memory of his uncle, Billy Duggan; Geoffrey Salvetti of the Palmerston Forts Association; Tony Clifford, Head of Classics at The Portsmouth Grammar School, for his translation of the inscriptions on the Hilsea Obelisk; Phil Loud, photographer of Southsea; and Errand Jervis Ltd, 63–65 Albert Road, Southsea, for their quick and efficient photocopying service which I have been using for a long time now.

I am very grateful for all the help I have received from the public archives and organisations and for permission to reproduce material from their collections: Portsmouth City Museum & Records Office including John Stedman, Jenny Stevens, Andrew Whitmarsh, the Military History Officer, Diana Gregg and all the staff in the Search Room; to Portsmouth City Council, in particular Myra Lee of the Engineering and Design Service, David Knight, the Leisure Officer, Bob Colley of the Planning Services, Ron Dooler, the Hilsea Lines Ranger, and Alan King, the Local Studies Librarian in the Norrish Central Library (Portsmouth).

Also my thanks go to Portsmouth Water for the supply of illustrations; the First Church of Christ, Scientist for the loan of photographs; the City of Portsmouth Preserved Transport Depot; Belinda Eastman of Mapped Out for the supply of maps; *The News*, Portsmouth, and Dr Anthony Morton, Archivist of the Royal Logistics Corps Museum for his help and assistance and the generous loan of archive materials. I am also grateful to the Illustrated London News Picture Library for permission to reproduce material and to the Ordnance Survey for permission to reproduce all the maps in this book.

I am also pleased and privileged to have permission from Garrick Palmer to include examples of his fine black and white photography and, in particular, a number of photographs which he has taken especially for this book.

Lastly, my thanks go to Steven Pugsley, the Chairman at Halsgrove, for putting Hilsea into print for the first time, and to everyone there for all their hard work.

Jane Smith (née Stark)
Southsea
February 2002

INTRODUCTION

*...One time I started from Common Hard, sailed past Southsea Castle, then
into Langstone Harbour; then struck my mast and went under Post Bridge
then set sail again and touched at Horsey Island, passed Portchester and Tipner
and then arrived at Common Hard again, thus making the compass of
Portsea Island in four hours, which island is seventeen miles in circumference...*

From: A Mariner of England: an Account of the Career of
William Richardson from Cabin Boy in the Merchant Service to
Warrant Officer in the Royal Navy (1780–1819) *as Told by Himself.*

The personality of Hilsea is unique but indefinable. It is a place which is sometimes water and sometimes land, it is located on Portsea Island but did not become part of Portsmouth until 1904. Sometimes, it was just left to lie as a rural hinterland. At others, it was fortified as a strategic military frontier. Bordered on two sides by Portsmouth Harbour, it never developed into a holiday resort in its own right, unlike its southern counterpart, Southsea. The building of Hilsea Lido and Stamshaw Esplanade in 1935 did, though, provide a seafront in the north for the first time. Following the construction of the M275 in the 1970s, the sight of boats in the water was replaced by the car over it; Hilsea became a place of perpetual movement against a backdrop of long-established communities and familiar landmarks.

Over the years, Hilsea's character established itself as an integral part of the favourite travelling rituals of every holidaymaker who ever drove over Portsdown Hill; catching their first glimpse of the sea from the top, down the old A3, past the Portsmouth Water Company building, over Portsbridge and on to Portsmouth and Southsea. On the way they looked out for their favourite landmarks, the Bastion Road House and the Southdown Bus Garage, the Hilsea Lido arch and tower, the Coach and Horses pub, and the United Services Garage.

So, while it may not be possible to pin down precisely the elusive nature of Hilsea's character, it is possible to separate out all the different strands of Hilsea's personality. But first, to set the scene...

Where is it?

The geographical character of Hilsea is defined by the meeting of land and water. It is situated in the north-west corner of Portsea Island and is surrounded by water on two sides. On the north side there is Portscreek (shown on some maps as Port Creek) which is part of Tipner Lake, and, on the west side, Tipner Lake itself, which is part of Portsmouth Harbour (North). Today, four bridges cross Portscreek over to the mainland of Hampshire. They are the main road bridge at the Portsbridge roundabout junction with the M27, another at the Eastern Road, a foot-bridge between Peronne Road and Highbury, and the railway bridge at Portcreek Junction.

Two forms of land transport converge at Hilsea, road and rail. Back in the 1930s when Portsmouth Airport was open, Hilsea could also be reached by air. Today, at the Portsbridge roundabout, three major roads converge from the west and north, the M27 motorway, the A27 (Western Road) and the A3 (Northern Road). On leaving the roundabout, these roads become the London Road, Portsmouth, which leads southwards down into the centre of the city. A traffic filter system then gives out on to Northern Parade on the west side and Copnor Road on the east side.

The railway line runs from the mainland, over Portcreek Junction, southwards to the main railway stations at Portsmouth & Southsea and Portsmouth Harbour. Hilsea has its own station just past Portcreek Junction.

As regards the water, Portsea Island and Portsmouth Harbour are part of the 12 harbours and estuaries which go to make up the estuarine complex of the Solent. The north-west corner of Hilsea borders the stretch of water between Tipner Bridge and Portsbridge roundabout which is known as Tipner Lake and occupies an area of 46 hectares of silty mud-land with a few permanent wet channels. Portscreek is also part of Tipner Lake and connects it with Langstone Harbour. Both the lake and Portscreek are part of Portsmouth Harbour (North). All this stretch of water is tidal, ensuring a continual change of scenery as tides ebb and flow. Portsmouth Harbour (North) is now an important Conservation Area, being a Site of Special Scientific Interest (SSSI) which supports a variety of wildlife.

Prior to the building of the M275, this water was navigable and it was possible to sail right round Portsea Island. Today, however, it would be almost impossible because of the restrictions of the Portsbridge roundabout and the limited height of the other bridges.

How Hilsea developed

Hilsea today consists of the heritage of seven quite distinct entities. The communities making up these entities have been superimposed on each other during the centuries, following political, military and social changes in the rest of the country. First of all came the rural society of its very early history, then the military personnel who constructed and inhabited the eighteenth-century fortifications of the Hilsea Lines, and later, the huge Hilsea Barracks and Rugby Camp site. Next came the late-Victorians who moved out to Portsmouth's suburbia when North End was extended and after them, the people who were rehoused in the large council estate created around Hilsea Crescent as part of the massive slum clearance programme in Portsea following the First World War.

Then came the people who moved into the brand new streets created in the major building expansion of the 1930s which also included Hilsea Lido. After the Second World War, another new community was formed as part of the post-war developments and re-use of redundant military sites. Lastly, when the housing stopped the gateway began – the buildings on either side of Portsbridge, such as the Southdown Bus Garage and the Portsmouth Water Company Booster Station at Cosham, created a set of familiar landmarks for people entering or leaving the City of Portsmouth.

The Heart of Hilsea

Demographically, the modern ward of Hilsea is 314 hectares in size with the largest population in the City of Portsmouth, its 16 300 people coming from all age groups. The ward is defined as having the typical characteristics of suburbia, with an unemployment rate of 3.4 per cent in 1998 as compared to the City in general of 5.25 per cent. Just over 4000 people commute daily into the ward to work, almost 5000 commute out to other areas, while 2000 both live and work in Hilsea.

There are five schools: the City of Portsmouth Boys' School, Gatcombe Park Infants' School, Northern Parade Infant/Junior School, Stamshaw Infants' School and Corpus Christi Roman Catholic Primary School. Its five places of worship are: St Francis' Church in Northern Parade, the Society of Friends Meeting House in Northwood Road, St Nicholas' Church in Battenburg Road, The First Church of Christ, Scientist in London Road, and Corpus Christi Roman Catholic Church in Gladys Avenue.

Of its nine pubs, five are Edwardian buildings: the Avenue Hotel in Twyford Avenue, the Green Posts in London Road, the Fountain also in London Road, the Spotted Cow in North End Avenue and the Portland in Stamshaw Road. Then come the three inter-war pubs: the Coach and Horses in London Road, The Oakwood, in Northern Parade, and the Phoenix in Torrington Road. Lastly, there is the Toby Carvery, which is a pub/restaurant conversion of a much older building.

The main leisure facilities include Alexandra Park, the Mountbatten Sports Centre and the Stamshaw Esplanade leading to Hilsea Lido, the Portsmouth Grammar School playing fields and the former Civil Service playing fields off the Copnor Road, now a health club.

Hilsea's architecture includes one Scheduled Ancient Monument and Conservation Area, known as the Hilsea Lines; four buildings Grade II Listed (i.e., of special architectural and historical interest which warrant every effort being made to preserve them), the Fountain pub, Hilsea's two eighteenth-century houses, Gatcombe House and a building in the London Road, and the former Green Farm farmhouse and barn, now part of the Toby Carvery. There are two Grade II Listed monuments, the Hilsea Obelisk and the milestone opposite the News Centre.

There are also four buildings by the well-known Portsmouth architect Arthur Edward Cogswell (1858–1934); these are the Avenue Hotel (1897), the Fountain Inn (1900), the Coach and Horses (1929) and St Nicholas' Church (1929–30).

The Illustrations

So, how can all these different elements possibly be brought together? The history of each of these groups is worthy of a major research project in its own right. However different they are though, the one factor that linked them in the past and links them still today is their shared location on the gateway to Portsmouth.

The purpose of this book then, is to bring all these aspects of Hilsea together for the first time and what better way to do it than by means of illustrations and photographs from a wide variety of sources. These include maps, photographs of family gatherings, events, captured in pictures taken by local reporters, particularly sporting events, photographs taken by individuals to record local buildings and familiar landmarks, and postcards produced by local firms of Hilsea's tourist attractions, the brand-new lido, pleasure park and seafront in the north. Most of these have never been published before and some have been specially commissioned for this book.

Hilsea is so familiar to its residents now that perhaps we can no longer see it. Its overall character has been diffused among its component parts for too long. Now, thanks to the people of the past who have had the foresight to record its characteristics, all its attributes can be gathered together to stand out in relief from the background.

We can stop, look around and enjoy what we see without having to hurry on through to somewhere else. While it is true to say that the complete history of Hilsea and its surroundings has yet to be written, we can, in this Golden Jubilee Year, look back over half a century of memories. For the first time, we can take the opportunity to look at the gateway to Portsmouth with fresh eyes.

For the purposes of this book, the boundary of Hilsea is defined as the modern ward boundary as shown on this map, date of map unknown.

COURTESY OF PORTSMOUTH CITY COUNCIL

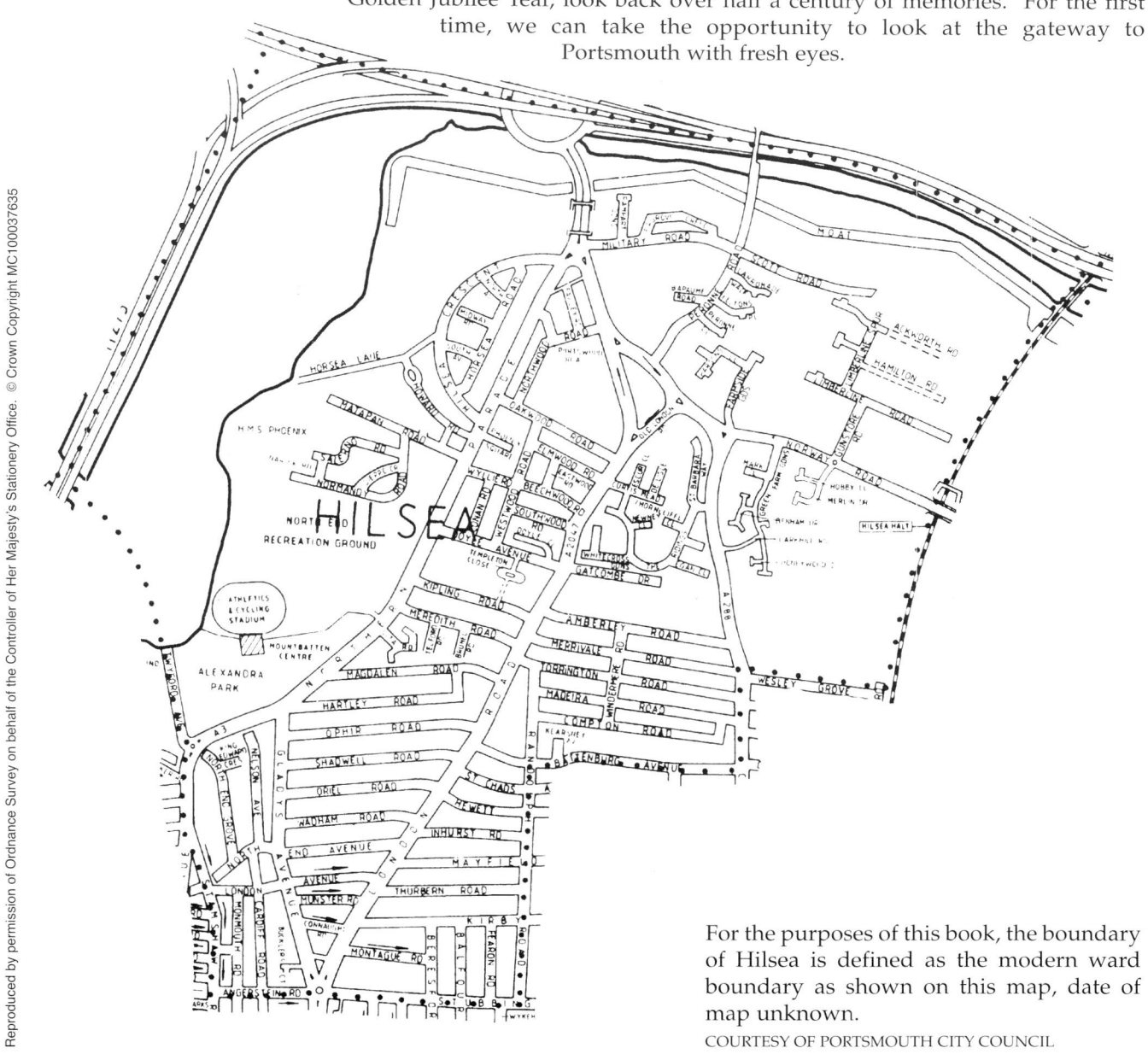

THE BOOK OF HILSEA

This map dated 1991 shows the boundaries of the City of Portsmouth which now include Portsea Island and parts of the mainland. It is divided into the neighbourhoods which it comprises. COURTESY OF PORTSMOUTH CITY COUNCIL

Chapter 1 1066–1500
THE LAND RAISED IN MARSH

The fate of Hilsea has been inextricably linked with the question of access from the mainland of Hampshire across to Portsea Island. In her book on the origins of Portsmouth, Sarah Quail has remarked that the island was not a particularly hospitable place in the late twelfth century as the way across was either by boat or causeway at low tide. In fact, the first reference to a bridge did not appear in the Pipe Rolls until the 1190s. Hilsea had actually existed long before the town of Portsmouth which was not founded until 1180, receiving its first Charter in 1194. However, it does not appear in the Domesday Book in its own right because it was part of the manor of Wymering on the mainland.

The population at this time was very small. The Domesday Book records a working male population of 74 for both Wymering and Cosham, with only 31 for the whole of Portsea Island. There were three manors on the island, Buckland, Copnor and Fratton, but they had few amenities. So, the old, Saxon Hilsea started life as a small hamlet situated in marshy, uninviting and remote countryside with scant population.

The place and the land on which it stood amounted to one and the same thing, as by the thirteenth century, the ancient West Saxon dialect name for Hilsea had been recorded as Helesye. This translates either as Holly Island, possibly referring to a plant which grew there or the 'raised land in marsh'. Other variants were 'Hulleseie' and 'Heleseye'. Nine centuries on, holly can still be found near the moat of the Hilsea Lines. (January 2002)

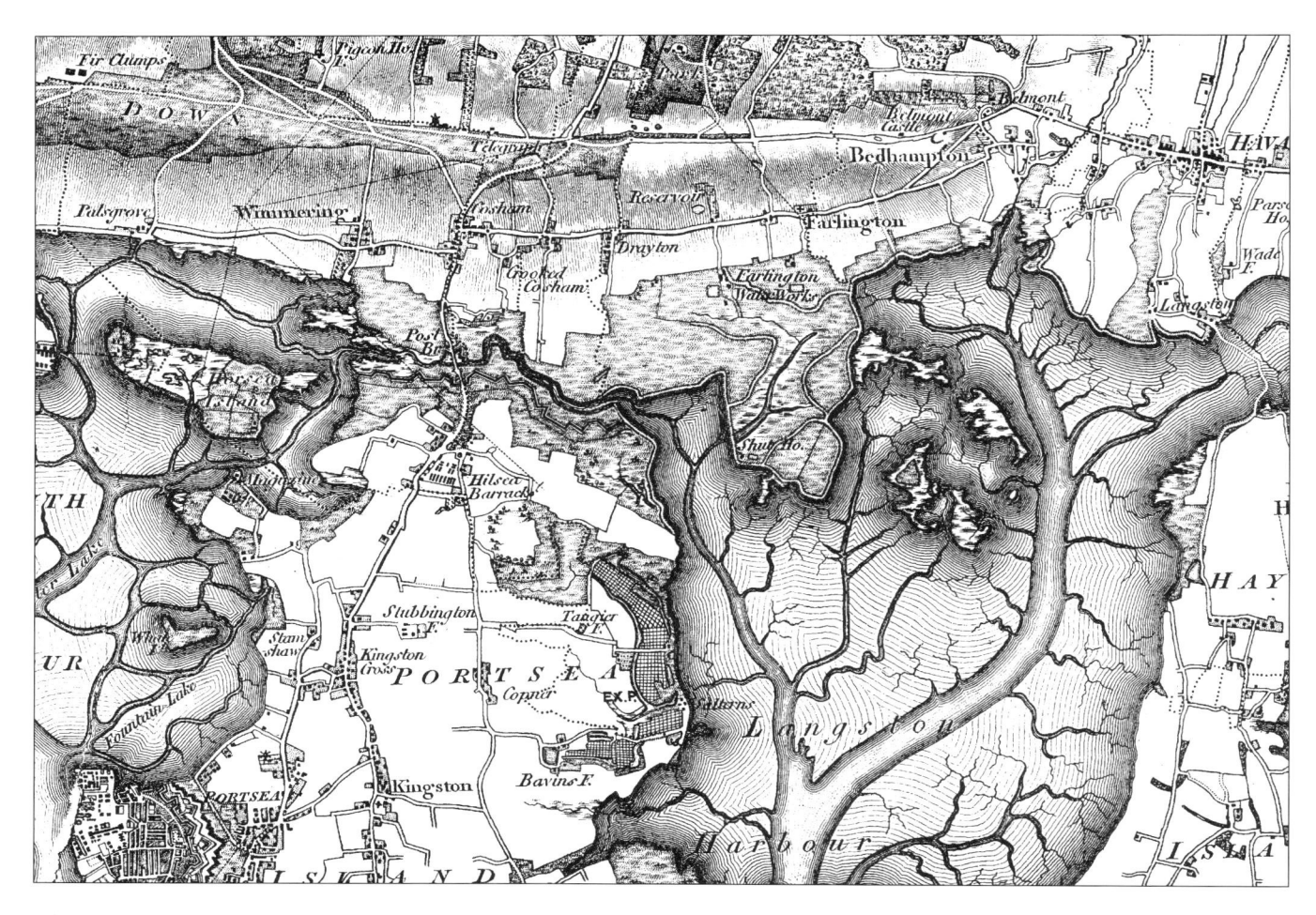

This picturesque map of the early 1800s shows Portsea Island and its surroundings: Portchester Castle can just been seen on the very far left and Hayling Island on the far right. The marshy nature of the north of Portsea Island and the creeks and lakes of the harbour have been beautifully drawn – such inhospitable terrain would obviously deter any invaders. Portsbridge is shown as Post Bridge and the fortifications either side of the bridge and the barracks stand out. The little hamlet of Hilsea clusters around the main fork of the one road on to the island and the rest of the countryside is quite rural. COURTESY OF MAPPING OUT

Chapter 2 1500–1900
RURAL HINTERLAND OR MILITARY FRONTIER?

By the times of the Tudors, Portsea Island consisted of a collection of agricultural villages with their population mostly involved in communal systems of farming. A large portion of the arable land formed what was known as common fields, containing the properties of the various owners. These lay scattered in a multitude of narrow strips known as furlongs. There were five groups of common fields on Portsea Island; Buckland and Kingston, Fratton, Copnor, Milton and Hilsea. The fact that Hilsea was linked administratively with Wymering on the mainland, meant that it had little in common with its neighbours.

John Chapman, in his Portsmouth Paper on the common lands of Portsea Island, has remarked that Hilsea's common pastures and common wastes were most extensive for a small village. Close to the village itself lay Hilsea Green which extended over 25 acres. As this was much larger than the traditional village green it could have been used for pasture. Both fields and common land were enclosed in 1815.

So, what happened to change the perception of Hilsea from that of rural hinterland of the mainland, with no connection with Portsmouth, to that of its military frontier? What differentiated the area from the very similar Hayling Island or the harbours of Langstone and Chichester? Once founded, the town of Portsmouth occupied a small area in the south-west corner of Portsea Island. It began as a fishing and trading centre but soon took on its role as a naval and military base and began to prosper and expand. Eventually, this expansion was to reach Hilsea and its rural character would be lost altogether.

Henry VII decided that Portsmouth, with its sheltered, protected and deep-water harbour should become the home of his navy. Henry VIII continued the work started by his father and with a chain of blockhouses along the coast began the massive construction work that was eventually to change Portsea Island into Fortress Portsmouth, and Hilsea into a fortified frontier.

Following the renewal of war with France in the 1750s, entrenchments were constructed along the southern side of Portscreek. These became the forerunner of the Hilsea Lines, Hilsea's most important and largest fortification. Their site was recognised then as being of great strategic importance to the defence of Portsmouth's Royal Dockyards from landward attack and remained so for over one hundred years. For the first time, the marshy and open landscape was seen as an advantage because invaders could be seen a long way off and had nothing to protect them during any invasion.

Fortifications though, meant soldiers and soldiers had to be quartered somewhere. A tiny hamlet like Hilsea could not be expected to accommodate them itself so barracks would have to be built. Hilsea's military connections date from 1587 when it was used as the training ground for volunteers who were to defend the naval port against the Spanish Armada should it land. A century later, under the Stuarts, a camp had been set up to hold a force ready for action overseas.

Temporary buildings were erected in 1756 on a site adjacent to the rural centre of Hilsea and occupied by the Royal Marine Light Infantry until 1783. Hilsea then became a transit depot and continued in this role until 1854. During this period, very many soldiers passed through with their units on their way to and from foreign service. In 1820, one of them was my own great-great-great-grandfather, a Sergeant in the King's Own Regiment who passed through Hilsea on his way to Portsmouth and then on to Waterford in Ireland.

In 1815, the buildings were used to house the wounded brought home from the Battle of Waterloo, many of these casualties dying and being buried within the perimeter of the barracks. However, in 1854 permanent buildings were constructed to house the troops, horses and guns of the Royal Field Artillery to man the fortifications which existed at that time on Portsdown Hill. The Royal Artillery had their home in Hilsea until 1921 when the barracks became the Depot of the Royal Army Ordnance Corps which had moved there from Woolwich. Hilsea Barracks served then as the RAOC School of Instruction and the basic training unit for National Service Recruits until it closed in 1962 and the site was converted to housing.

The Hilsea Obelisk

The obelisk knows rather more about Portsmouth than Portsmouth knows about it. William Gates in his book on Portsmouth's past, states that the site of the obelisk was originally known as Shawecross. However, nothing is known about the significance of its combination of inscriptions and its own date, its stonemason, or its date and place of manufacture; Portsmouth City Council does not even own the land it stands on.

Hilsea's most important monument is Grade II Listed and is situated on the junction of Torrington Road and the east side of the London Road. This obelisk is mounted on a square base with mouldings, its west face bearing one crest in relief, two incised inscriptions and one inscription on a plaque. The crest is the Crest of Portsmouth, the new moon cradling the dog star Sirius. The first Latin inscription, BURGI DE PORTESMOUTH LIBERIATIM LIMES, translates as Boroughs of Portsmouth Boundary of Liberties. Another Latin inscription, ANNO DOMINI MDCCXCIX REV GEO CUTHBERT PR*ETORE, means, In the year of the Lord 1799 Reverend Geo Cuthbert Magistrate — in classical Latin the asterisk replaces the letter 'a'. Lastly, there is an inscription on a plaque in English, 'This stone marks the boundary of Portsmouth prior to the extension of 1832'. (February 2002)

Old Rural Hilsea

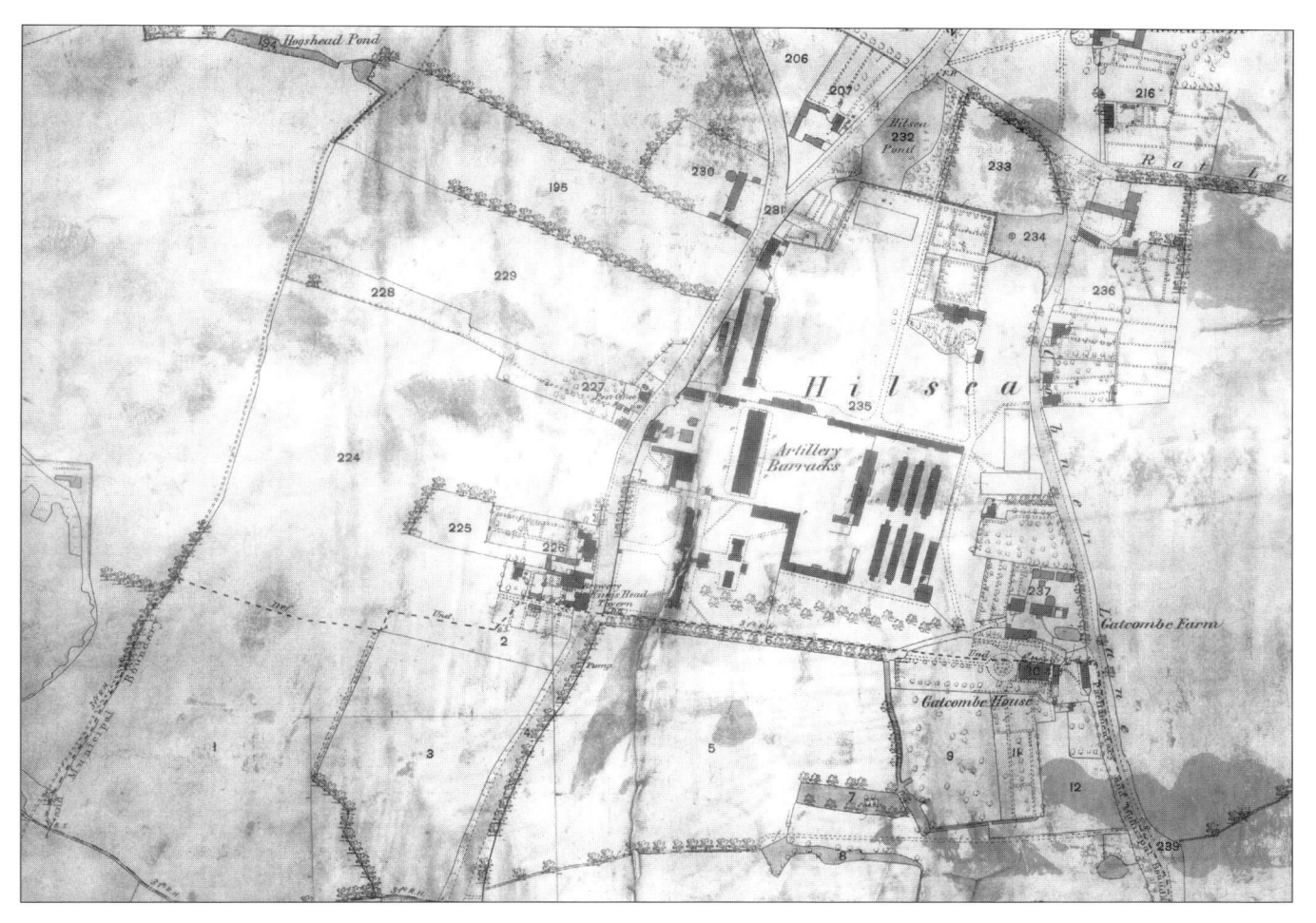

This map, dating from the 1860s, shows the centre of ancient rural Hilsea and the adjacent Artillery Barracks. Three ponds are clearly shown: Hilsea Pond at no. 232, the pond opposite Green Farm at no. 234 and the Hogshead Pond in the top left-hand corner at no. 194. This lay in what was to become Northern Parade and local people still recall problems with the marshy land there. COURTESY OF PORTSMOUTH COUNCIL

This milestone, which still stands in the London Road, reckons the mileage from the extremity of Point, off Broad Street, Old Portsmouth; London: 66 miles, Petersfield: 14 and Portsmouth 3. Originally one of a group of six, one disappeared but the others still stand modestly performing their function amid the hustle and bustle of life today and serving as a reminder to us of a much more ancient and slower way of life. It is a Grade II Listed monument but its actual age is unknown. (November 2001)

The milestone is marked on this map, dating from the 1860s, along with the Coach and Horses pub and Hilsea Farm. Rat Lane is now Norway Road.
COURTESY OF PORTSMOUTH CITY COUNCIL

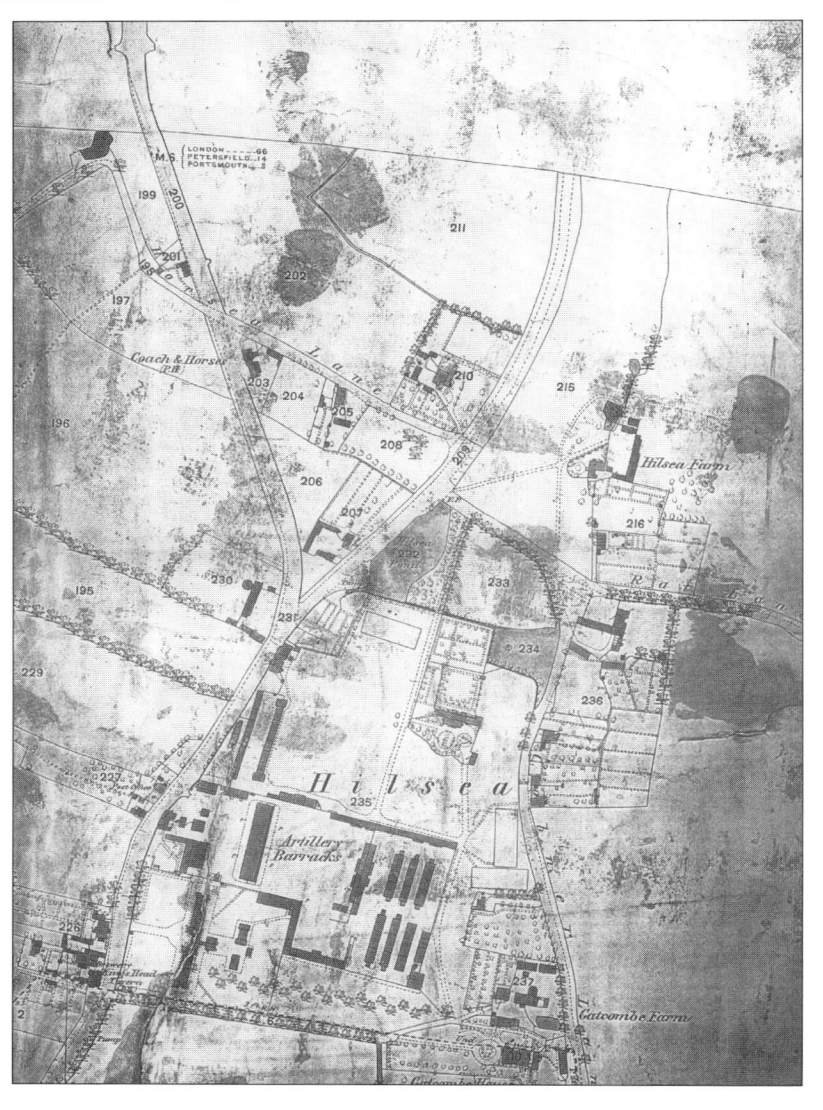

The last vestige of old rural Hilsea, Green Farm was the last working farm on Portsea Island. Believed to date from 1630, it originally consisted of 40 acres of land which stretched as far as the railway line and was owned by the War Department who maintained the buildings. The land was eventually sold off and by 1989 it had been reduced to barely one and a half acres. The farmhouse was once a group of cottages with one end of it added at a later date, and in 1980, a well 18ft deep was discovered in the garden. The farm was known locally as 'the rhubarb farm' because of the amount of rhubarb which grew there. The Benham family farmed it from 1933 to 1962 but in the 1990s, the land was sold and it was converted into a bar and restaurant called the Toby Carvery. Its old form is still easily recognisable and both the farmhouse and barn are Grade II Listed. (November 2001)

The barn has the date of 1840 on it and originally was one of several. The other remaining barn blew down in the hurricane of 1987. The last barn is also part of the conversion and a road running alongside called Green Farm Gardens retains the memory of its rural past. (November 2001)

This picture shows the rustic design of the Coach and Horses pub after it has just been rebuilt after having been damaged by fire in 1870. It was originally an old coaching inn situated at the junction of Copnor Road to the left and London Road to the right. As it was the first inn encountered on entering Portsea Island it has become a very familiar landmark and almost symbolic of Hilsea in its own right. The illustration on the wall with the order, 'Stand and deliver!' relates to a story that when the owner purchased the premises from the War Office he was charged what he considered to be such an exorbitant price that he likened it to highway robbery! COURTESY J.A. HEWES

Illustration complete! Portsmouth Guildhall can just be made out in the background. COURTESY J.A. HEWES

Military Hilsea and The Hilsea Lines

...I was staying at Fareham Keeping a Hare Dressing Shop and was doing very well, but threw a Distervance braking out at manchester the whole of the viterns was called out we Apeard at Andover to be inspected by the doctor. I was ordered to hilsey Barracks near Portsmouth to join the 2nd viterans we was sent from Portsmouth to Waterford in Ireland and their i made up my 21 years and 3 months and I came Intitled to 1s 10 pr day...

From: James Carsley, His Story, 1820.

Below: The *Illustrated London News*, a very popular paper in its day, runs a feature, dated 1882, on the Hilsea Lines and shows the fortifications being viewed by military men and their ladies dressed in fashionable outfits. They make quite a contrast with the bleak, desolate character of this part of Hilsea, now specifically designed as a no-man's land and part of the defences of Portsmouth.

COURTESY ILLUSTRATED LONDON NEWS PICTURE LIBRARY

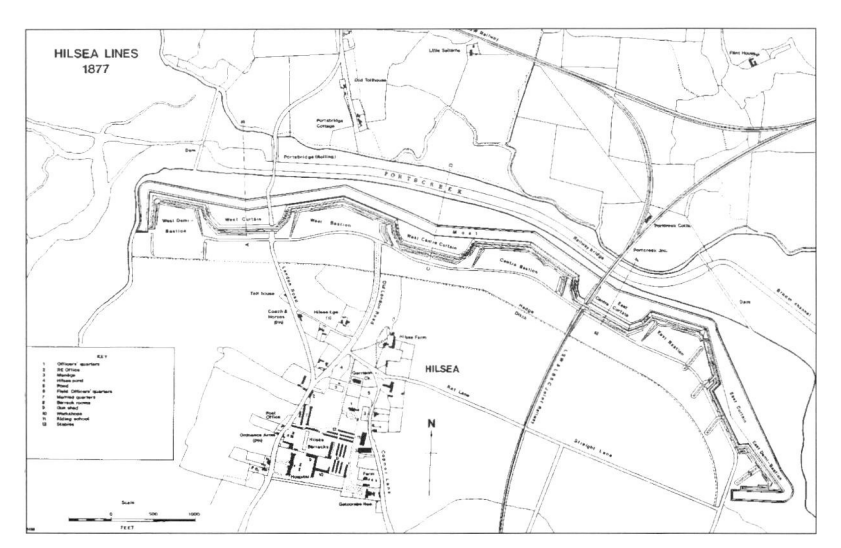

The term Lines is a common one for fortifications – there is one in Chatham, for example – and derives from the lines of tents in a military encampment. The bastions were constructed at Hilsea in 1860 and this map, dated 1877, shows the details of their formation and connects rural Hilsea to military Hilsea. The railway has now reached Portsea Island, by means of a tunnel constructed through the fortifications. The barracks are gradually expanding and the garrison church has now been built. The London Road has been rerouted to run directly down to Portsbridge but the old London Road is still shown.
COURTESY G.H. MITCHELL

The Hilsea Arches controlled the entrance to Portsea Island and were constructed in 1861. Here, a tram just about fits underneath on its way to Cosham and Portsbridge can be glimpsed through the arch. They were demolished in 1919.

A tram wends its way through old rural Hilsea towards Cosham with the barracks on the left. The buildings on the left were demolished when the barracks were extended.

The London Road and its Houses

Each side of the London Road and their side turnings were the first areas to be built up. A notable feature was the size of the houses on corner sites, along with equally large gardens. Some do survive, but most have been converted into flats or offices with the gardens cemented over. A very fine example that does remain is St Hilda's, built in 1883. (January 2002)

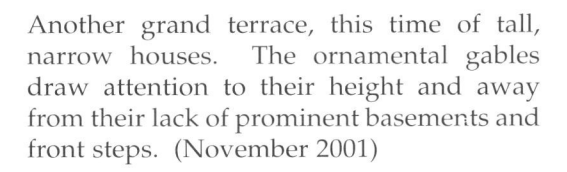

A closer view of St Hilda's, its country-cottage style of architecture illustrating very clearly how this part of Hilsea was considered to be a rural retreat from urban North End. (January 2002)

Another grand terrace, this time of tall, narrow houses. The ornamental gables draw attention to their height and away from their lack of prominent basements and front steps. (November 2001)

Mornington Terrace, London Road. Well-to-do residents who could afford several servants and wanted to move out from the crowded centre of North End but could not quite stretch to a large detached corner property, could choose a house in an imposing terrace like this one. Its name carries overtones of Mornington Crescent, the elegant London address near Regent's Park. Each house had two storeys as well as basements and attic rooms for the servants. (November 2001)

Chapter 3 1880–1914
PORTSMOUTH'S LATE-VICTORIAN SUBURBIA

'Battle of Minden'

A well-known inn and coaching house at Hilsea which has long since disappeared. It used to boast a signboard painted by Sir Robert Kerporter. About the middle of the eighteenth century it gained unenviable notoriety, its proprietor, Samuel James Lewis, being robbed and murdered by a sergeant of the Royal Marines named Williams, who was tried at Winchester, convicted and hanged on Southsea Common in 1768. His gibbeted body was taken down and buried secretly by his comrades, the mystery of its disappearance being solved twenty years later, when the remains were found during some excavations on the fortifications.

From Portsmouth in the Past *by William G. Gates.*

The boundaries of Hilsea overlap with its neighbours to the south and west. To the south, North End covers the area of Kingston Cross to the Green Posts pub opposite Torrington Road, and to the west, Stamshaw covers the area between Gladys Avenue and Stamshaw Road. Both areas were built up before Hilsea and the design of their layout greatly influenced that of Hilsea when it came to be finally developed in the 1920s and '30s.

Portsmouth expanded all through the 1800s and although the ancient farm land was gradually built over, the design of the new residential areas was not just random. The shape of the urban expansion was dictated by the lines of the ancient strips of the common fields. At first glance, the map of North End can just appear to be a geometric grid but in fact, many roads, such as Pitcroft Road for example, now just over the border from modern Hilsea, are curved. This curve was typical of the rural strips which had to allow for the turning of the plough teams.

The main development of the London Road occurred between the 1880s and 1913. By 1900, houses had reached The Green Posts pub and Magdalen Road. Hilsea was regarded as the rural end of Portsmouth and well-to-do families moved out into the large houses to get away from the more densely populated centre of Portsmouth. Stamshaw, however, was developed as rows and rows of terraced houses for dockyard workers built almost up to the First World War. A plaque on a house in Angerstein Road records the building of Coronation Terrace in 1911, the year of the coronation of King George V and Queen Mary. A smart new hotel was built in 1897 at its northern point near the sea, the Avenue Hotel in Twyford Avenue, designed by Arthur Cogswell.

North End is, of course, known for its multitude of shops and was the nearest shopping centre to Hilsea. The man who played a large part in this initial commercial growth in North End was A.W. White, who lived in a house called The Poplars situated at the apex of the Gladys Avenue and London Road junction, now replaced by an office building. This building was originally the office of the Southsea Tourist Co. built in 1923. Southdown took over this company in 1925 and it remained a busy office until fairly recently. In 1879, he established Portsmouth's own tramway system which ran through to Southsea and its shops. In 1883, when Gladys Avenue was constructed, he was allowed to name it after his daughter Gladys. Mr White also ran a furniture repository business with premises just on the border of modern Hilsea on the corner of Stubbington Avenue.

While in general, the late-Victorians and Edwardians were happy to build over Hilsea's rural past, they did retain something of its history. The old coaching inns, the Fountain and the Green Posts in the London Road, were rebuilt in the early 1900s. The Fountain was also designed by Arthur Cogswell who actually lived in North End himself, in a house called 'Sunnicote', today numbered 161 London Road.

No Edwardian development would be complete without a park of course, and in 1907, Alexandra Park was opened. Originally, it had a bandstand, trees, flower beds and a pavilion and it gave Hilsea its first public amenity, one that is still very popular today.

The London Road and its Houses

Even the more modest terraced houses built in the side roads branching off the London Road had their own decorative wrought iron porches. This is a feature of terraced houses in Portsmouth generally and the green one on the end is a particularly fine example. (November 2001)

The houses which finally reached the old boundary of Hilsea and Portsmouth at Torrington Road marked the end of the building of Portsmouth's late-Victorian new suburbia just before the First World War. This house has the date 1900, a very fine decorative portico and a house name, 'Halifax' displayed prominently on ornamental glass. House names which evoked country-house grandeur were very much a feature of Portsmouth and Southsea and this fashion was continued in Hilsea. Names such as 'Alexandra', 'St Hilary', 'Mentmore' and 'Glenroyde' and my favourite, 'Rustic Dene', can still be seen on many houses today. (November 2001)

The Green Posts pub was a coaching inn taking its name from the boundary of the ancient Borough of Portsmouth which was originally a green post. Now, it is the second pub on the London Road after the Coach and Horses and this building dates from the 1900s. It is situated opposite the obelisk at the corner of Torrington Road which marks the old northern limits of Portsmouth and presumably replaced the post. (November 2001)

The Fountain pub, which was also a very old coaching inn, was rebuilt in 1900 to a design by Arthur Cogswell for the brewery Messrs Pike, Spicer & Co. It is Grade II Listed, one of its features being the green and brown glazed tiles on the facade. (February 2002)

The Border with Stamshaw

The glazed tiles continue on a row of terraced houses between the London Road and the western boundary of Hilsea along Stamshaw Road. Tiled facades are a feature of other terraces in Portsmouth. (February 2002)

A lovely example of an Edwardian ornamental portico displaying a stained glass window with a house name in Edwardian lettering surrounded by a stylish Art Nouveau design. The black and white colour scheme is very unusual, as are the diamond window panes. The double-front doors are seen often in Portsmouth and Southsea. (February 2002)

A vista along North End Avenue with its variety of architecture showing Stamshaw Infant School on the right which was built in 1899. Its large windows and single storey are typical of early school buildings. (February 2002)

Stamshaw Infant School from the east showing its belfry which is an unusual feature. Its date, 1899, can be seen on the plaque on the gable in the centre. (February 2002)

Just opposite the school is the Spotted Cow, a pub built in 1900 to a design by A.H. Bone, another well-known Portsmouth architect. (February 2002)

The Portland pub, built in the 1890s, lies right on the border of Hilsea and Stamshaw. This modest one-storey pub boasts a cosy interior with an ornamental fireplace. Originally it was known as the Portland Arms. (February 2002)

Corpus Christi Roman Catholic Church in Gladys Avenue was built in 1893. There is now a primary school attached to it. (February 2002)

At the junction of Twyford Avenue and what was to become Northern Parade stands the Avenue Hotel, another Cogswell pub built for Messrs Pike, Spicer & Co. in 1897. A very imposing building, it was designed to contrast with the terraced houses nearby and must have done good business when the cycle track and then Alexandra Park opened immediately opposite. (February 2002)

Alexandra Park Opens

Alexandra Park was named in honour of Princess Alexandra, Princess of Wales who had become Queen Alexandra on the death of Queen Victoria in 1901. It was designed as the sister park to Victoria Park which had been laid out in the centre of Portsmouth in 1878. A cycle track had already been constructed on the site by H.P. Boulnois, Borough Engineer from 1883–1900. This was considered to be quite an innovation in its time because of its banked sides. The park was opened on 27 June 1907. The date of this photograph is unknown although the lovely Edwardian dresses and hats reveal it to have been taken before 1914. It shows the unveiling ceremony of the clock on the pavilion by Councillor Sir J. Timpson. The clock is no longer in existence and the pavilion was rebuilt in 1939 and completed in March 1940. COURTESY OF PORTSMOUTH CITY MUSEUM & RECORDS SERVICE

ALEXANDRA PARK

THIS PARK WAS FORMALLY OPENED
ON THE 27TH JUNE, 1907, BY
THE MAYOR.
(COUNCILLOR C. DYE)
THE WORK OF LAYING IT OUT WAS ENTRUSTED BY
THE PARKS AND OPEN SPACES COMMITTEE TO THE
SUB-COMMITTEE FOR THE NORTHERN DIVISION.
COMPOSED OF :-
ALDERMAN C. JENKINS, CHAIRMAN.
ALDERMAN F. POWER, COUNCILLORS T. BREWIS,
H. W. BLACKADAR, H. KIMBER, J.P.,
H. PALIN, F. PEARCE, C. F. SAUNDERS,
AND S. E. SPRIGINGS.

A plaque commemorating the opening of the park. The plaque itself looks modern but the stone surround and City Crest could date from 1907. (February 2002)

The original park lodge situated next to the main gates. The lodge and the plaque stonework are the only remaining original parts of Alexandra Park still surviving. (February 2002)

Chapter 4 1919–1939
A NEW LIFE AROUND HILSEA CRESCENT

...When I first came to the house in 1929 aged 6, I was frightened of the bath.
We were used to a bath in front of the fire and my mother just couldn't get me into it!

Elsie Craigie talking to me, 7 August 2001

The Hilsea Crescent estate was built from 1926 onwards at the northern end of Northern Parade and consisted of five roads, Hilsea Crescent, Horsea Road, Midway Road and North and South Avenues. The estate was built on former allotment ground so its design was not influenced by the ancient field strips. The houses were laid out in the shape of a crescent with its ends enclosed by Northern Parade.

During the inter-war years, Portsmouth City Council embarked on a massive slum clearance programme in Portsea, in the centre of Portsmouth. Previously, families had lived in tiny 'two-up, two-down' terraced cottages, with no running water or toilets. At last, these homes were condemned as unfit for human habitation and demolished. The families were moved to the brand new houses in Hilsea where they had a good-sized three-bedroomed house with a bathroom and their own gardens at front and back.

Other facilities though, took time to arrive. As the nearest shops were either over Portsbridge at Cosham or in Stamshaw, one lady opened a small shop in her own kitchen. The Hilsea Market shopping parade in the London Road was built in the 1930s and did provide a group of shops selling essential items. The nearest school was also in Stamshaw until the Northern Parade Infant and Junior School in Kipling Road was built in 1930. The local Brownie Pack would meet at the community centre in Northern Parade known as St Joan's which at this time was just a wooden hut on bricks. These were the years of the Depression and many men were out of work so a soup kitchen was set up at St Joan's which provided jugs of soup for needy families.

Public transport was limited as Northern Parade itself was not built up until the 1930s. Even the tramway system never came as it was due to be replaced by trolley buses. Eventually, in 1935, Hilsea Crescent was linked to the centre of Portsmouth when the trolley-bus system was extended to run from Commercial Road to Cosham via Twyford Avenue, Alexandra Park and Hilsea.

During the 1930s, the eastern side of Northern Parade was built up as the roads linking it to the London Road appeared. The Oakwood pub was built at the end of Oakwood Road and the old community centre replaced by St Francis' Church next door. The church was built entirely of brick and to raise money for its construction, local residents could buy a brick for one shilling (5p). To celebrate the coronation of King George VI and Queen Elizabeth, the late Queen Mother, in 1937, a group of houses known as the Coronation Eventide Homes were built in 1938. These were designed by Adrien Sharp, Portsmouth's first City Architect who had been appointed in 1936.

For local children, there was Alexandra Park with its children's playground just off Northern Parade and North End Recreation Ground. The greatest asset to the area was the development of the Hilsea Lido pleasure park during the 1930s and local children spent as much time there as they could.

In the pre-war years, Northern Parade ran alongside mostly open land with fields, trees and allotments. The rear of Hilsea Crescent opened out on to the foreshore and although construction work to build a seawall and esplanade was begun in 1936, it was not completed until 1938. Horsea Lane, known as Piggery Lane, led down to the sea where, at low tide, it was possible to walk along one of the ancient wadeways over to Horsea Island where pigs were kept. It was also possible, in a way inconceivable today, to walk around the shoreline to Portchester Castle. Over to the east, Portsbridge was a pleasant place for walks, swimming and fishing.

In 1931, a large area of land between Hilsea Crescent and the Hilsea Lines was purchased by the Portsmouth Grammar School after years of negotiation with the government and the City Council for use as playing fields. It is still in use by the school today, thus ensuring that the area has always remained as unbuilt-up open space.

This map, dating from the 1930s, shows how the rural nature of Hilsea had by this time almost disappeared. Hilsea Crescent and its enclosed roads have now been built off what has become the Northern Parade and the roads linking Northern Parade and the London Road have now appeared. The area between North End Recreation Ground and the Crescent however, is still allotments. The wadeways can be clearly seen leading over to Horsea Island and at one time, were strengthened with stepping stones. The pot-boilers' referred to, found in 1925, are stones used by early man for heating up water for cooking. Note that the children's playground in Alexandra Park is situated off Northern Parade at this time. COURTESY OF MAPPED OUT

The look of the Hilsea Crescent area in January 2002 has hardly changed since it was built and it is still a very popular place to live.

The Northern Parade Community Centre is shown awaiting demolition. It was finally demolished in March 2002 after many years of being the focus for the social activities of the local community. (January 2002)

The Hilsea Market shops in the London Road were built in the early 1930s and were the nearest to Hilsea Crescent.
(January 2002)

Mrs Elsie Craigie was one of the first Brownies in Hilsea and is pictured (right) with her friend Daphne Hadley (left) in 1934. They are standing in the grounds of St Francis' Church Youth Centre in Northern Parade with the former Ministry of Defence houses of York Terrace in the background. They were members of the Imps' Six whose song was, 'We're the ever helpful Imps, quick and quiet as any shrimps'! This was sung as they danced around the toadstool in the Brownie circle.

Chapter 5 **1927**
THE NEW PORTSBRIDGE

The ford or wadeway across Portscreek was eventually replaced by single-span wooden or stone structures. In 1867, as part of the defences of Portsea Island, this simple design of bridge was replaced by what could be described as a horizontal drawbridge. The aim was to allow Portsea Island to be completely cut off from the rest of Hampshire should the mainland be invaded. A rolling bridge about 140ft long was installed which could be winched back and forth horizontally. A gap about 60ft wide was left to allow for the passage of gun boats between Portsmouth Harbour, along Portscreek to Langstone Harbour, to take supporting fire to wherever it might be needed.

Once the Hilsea Lines defence system had become redundant and the Hilsea Arches had been demolished in 1919, there was no longer the need to isolate Portsea Island in this way. In 1927, this rolling bridge was removed and replaced by an iron and concrete structure which remained until the widening of the Portsbridge roundabout in 1969.

A very rare view of the old rolling bridge, probably dating from the early 1900s. The mechanism can be seen on the middle pillar just below the tram going over the bridge towards Cosham. This bridge also had a walkway for pedestrians along its east side. The boy perched on the stonework is an unusual detail. COURTESY OF JOHN BOWRING

A very different Portsbridge is seen here with its stone pillars filled in and a causeway built on either side. There are two lamp columns on each side and a police box can just be seen on the Cosham end on the left. The moat was known as Hilsea Lagoon at this time and the Hilsea Lido site is just beginning to be developed. The putting green has appeared on the right and the tennis courts on the left but the edges of the moat are still looking unkempt. This is the design of Portsbridge that would now last until it was widened in 1969. The sender of this postcard has very thoughtfully dated it 9 September 1933!

Chapter 6 1930–1935
ART DECO HITS HILSEA

*Art Deco architecture was an architecture of ornament,
geometry, energy, retrospection, optimism,
colour, texture, light and at times even symbolism.*

Patricia Bayer from Art Deco House Style, *2001.*

Once the First World War had come and gone, it was obvious that Hilsea's military importance would never be the same again. By this time, the Hilsea Lines had been long redundant, having lost their place in the military strategic planning of the day. The Hilsea Arches had been demolished, Portsbridge had been re-designed and the Royal Artillery had been replaced at Hilsea Barracks by the Royal Army Ordnance Corps. Back in 1904, Hilsea had become a part of the Borough of Portsmouth which itself had become a city in 1927. The stage was set for the next major development. This would replace the military fortifications with a new leisure complex, continue the house building that had stopped short at Magdalen Road and give Hilsea its distinctive thirties' character which would last right through the Second World War until the 1960s.

Between 1919 and 1939, four million houses were built in Britain. A suburban home became more attainable to greater numbers of people than ever before. Most houses now had a living room, known as the front room, a dining room, known as the back room, a kitchen, three bedrooms and a bathroom. Electricity and gas supplies were laid on, along with hot and cold running water. Houses now had front and back gardens, however small, and roads and pavements were built up as the houses were constructed. The major difference between the inter-war years' residential developments and those built before the First World War was that, apart from council house construction, the building was still speculative but carried out on a much larger scale. More people could now not only afford a mortgage but were willing to take one on and wanted a new house which was easy to maintain and clean, of a size more appropriate to smaller families. This change in fashion happened to coincide with another major change in architectural style which could easily be applied to mass production – the emergence of Art Deco.

Art Deco was a type of architecture which had originally developed in France between the years 1908 and 1912. It became the latest fashion, reaching every Western country with its high point from 1925 to 1935. Originally known as the 'style moderne', it was a reaction to and development from the Art Nouveau style which was favoured by the Edwardians. It came in two main forms, the highly elaborate and stylised forms of decoration which contrasted with a more streamlined, geometric approach in which 'less is considered more'.

Houses designed in Art Deco or Modern Movement styles were very popular during the inter-war years, such as the Sunspan house on Portsdown Hill, with its white walls and flat roof. Others were built in Lee-on-Solent, Bognor Regis and Angmering-on-Sea. Although Hilsea did not have any white-walled Modern Movement houses, its builders did make the best use of the material that was most ready to hand for construction of all kinds on Portsea Island and that was brick.

The two dominant Art Deco styles of the inter-war years are not only demonstrated very clearly in Hilsea but remain almost intact from when they were first built. The flamboyant, inventive and almost theatrical side of Art Deco is represented in the usage of brick on houses, shops and other buildings; the streamlined, horizontal forms, also known as the International Style, can be seen in the Hilsea Lido swimming bath complex and the Southdown Bus Garage.

Art Deco had a short burst of glory. House building stopped when the Second World War broke out in 1939 and was not resumed again until the late 1940s. By that time Art Deco in all its forms had fallen out of fashion, but it did last long enough for Hilsea to benefit from its lively, dramatic and spontaneous influence.

A very early example of flamboyant Art Deco contrasting strongly with its neighbours and with its date on the facade. This building was originally intended as a church but is now used by the local Chinese community. (February 2002)

The Odeon in North End was built in 1936 and designed by architect Andrew Mather. While not strictly in Hilsea, it is included as it was the nearest cinema. This study by Garrick Palmer illustrates its distinctive style of lettering which was an important part of the house style of the Odeon cinema chain. The thin colour bands, in this case a light leaf-green, are also very typical as is the geometric, yet flowing design on the facade. The North End cinema is obviously designed to fit a small space, enlivening but not overpowering its surroundings.
(January 2002)

Situated right on the northern boundary of Hilsea in Stubbington Avenue, this shop was formerly the removal firm, A.H. White's, and is now Fads Home Care. Photographed by Garrick Palmer, its huge porticos and lines of large windows appear to move vertically and horizontally at the same time. This is a striking example of 'Departmental store Art-Deco'. The building has only a small part of its facade on the London Road, the rest is tucked away down Stubbington Avenue. The exotic design may have been influenced by the discovery of the Tomb of Tutenkhamun in 1922 as following that, elements of Egyptian art were introduced into Art Deco style. (January 2002)

This photograph by Garrick Palmer of a former department store in the London Road is built in the very distinctive International Style of the 1930s. Its streamlined, horizontal design with its balcony, sundeck and nautical overtones, shows that modern architectural styles had crossed the boundary with North End and had reached Hilsea. It looks very striking compared to the older style shops next to it. As with Fads Home Care, the design makes the most of a rather cramped corner site. Now, the shop is called Willows. (November 2001)

This smart building in the London Road is a thirties' design in brickwork and presents a complete contrast to the Art Deco architecture. (November 2001)

Battenburg Avenue, off the London Road, acquired a new church designed by the well-known Portsmouth architect Arthur Cogswell which was built in 1929/30. Its style is reminiscent of Hilsea's rural past and unique on Portsea Island. (January 2002)

This building stands next to the Green Posts pub and the brickwork has been left exposed to make it a feature of the building. The two curved columns appear to soften the severe horizontal facade and illustrate the versatility of brick. (November 2001)

The parade of shops opposite Kipling Road and on the junction with Merrivale Road – the block on the far right is called Merrivale Buildings. All of the shops are very long established. (November 2001)

Kipling Road looking west, one of a group of roads named after famous authors with Portsmouth connections who had died since 1900: Kipling Road, Meredith Road, Doyle Avenue and Conan Road, with Wyllie Road being named after the famous Portsmouth marine artist. As there was a brickworks nearby in Copnor, the material was easily available for use in the style both functional and decorative that is a prominent feature of houses not only in Hilsea but in Portsmouth and Southsea generally. Here, the curved garden walls make an attractive vista. (November 2001)

A very unusual feature of Hilsea and Portsea Island is these brick-built backways with brick-walled gardens and angled garages. While the back gardens are small, these high walls give them more privacy than might be expected in such a densely built-up area. Unlike many places, these localities have hardly changed in half a century. (November 2001)

The rear entrance of the Northern Parade Infants' and Junior School which was built in the 1930s to cater for all the children in the newly built residential area. Again, the brickwork of this one-storey building is very prominent. (February 2002)

Northern Parade and Its Features

A vista along Northern Parade which was built up in the 1930s. An interesting feature of this part is the flats built broadside on to the road. (February 2002)

Another vista along Northern Parade with a terrace of bow windows. (February 2002)

Stained glass windows with Art Deco designs are a feature of 1930s houses. Here is a most attractive swallow. (February 2002)

These modest two-storey buildings are known as the Coronation Eventide Homes, having been opened in 1938, the year after the coronation of George VI and Queen Elizabeth (the late Queen Mother). They were designed by the city architect Adrien Sharp, who was appointed in 1936. Miss Zetta Hill, shown on page 67 demonstrating her special water cycle at Hilsea Lido on 13 September 1937, also rode it a year later across the Solent from Ryde to Portsmouth to raise money for these Eventide Homes. Steamer trips had been arranged to allow the crowds to sail alongside her as she pedalled and the profits came to £12, a sizeable sum in 1938. Apparently she had made no allowance for the tides and the journey took six hours! (February 2002)

St Francis' Church in Northern Parade, again made of brick, built in 1936. (February 2002)

The Oakwood pub, also built in 1936, is one of Hilsea's two inter-war pubs, both built in a Neo-Georgian style with their brickwork as a decorative feature. They contrast dramatically with the flamboyant Edwardian buildings. (February 2002)

The Phoenix, Hilsea's second inter-war pub, occupies the site at the corner of Torrington Road and Windermere Road. Named after the naval establishment situated between Hilsea Crescent and Tipner Lake, it is an under-stated yet very attractive brick-built pub with its date, 1937, included in the decoration. (February 2002)

The Coach and Horses

The London Road approach to the Coach and Horses pub which was rebuilt in 1929 and completed in 1931 to a design by A.E. Cogswell for the Portsmouth and Brighton United Breweries. It is interesting that Cogswell chose a theatrical element of Art Deco, opting for a 'thirties' baronial' style (allegedly after a holiday in Scotland) rather than repeating the rustic-cottage style of the old building, thereby disguising its origins in old rural Hilsea.

He made picturesque use of a triangular site at an important junction, including an octagonal tower, a battlemented roofline, gables and small turrets. The external walls are in hard red brick and echo the fortifications at Portsbridge, some of which had recently been demolished. (November 2001)

It is now a popular pub and restaurant. The illustration 'Stand and Deliver' was recreated in decorative tiling and can be seen over the main door, and repeated on the other side of the building. Apparently, the Coach and Horses was the last major building designed by Cogswell which he saw completed in his lifetime.

Much older than the pub, this horse trough sits quietly alongside the London Road instructing 'Be kind to dumb animals'. It was passed into the ownership of Portsmouth City Council in 1905 but its age is unknown. (February 2002)

A shopping parade called Walberant Buildings was constructed just around the corner from the Coach and Horses in the 1930s. The main entrance with its curved glass window is reminiscent of the A.W. White's building in North End.
(February 2002)

'The Tower' house was designed to echo the now long-gone fortifications with its miniature battlements, elongated windows and military-style front door. It makes a good observation post, so to speak, at the end of the road. (February 2002)

The shopping parade's brick facade has centre sets of windows and a slight but subtle curve giving an illusion of depth to the frontage. (February 2002)

Hilsea Market is situated in the London Road near the milestone and also has long-established shops. (February 2002)

A brick tour de force continuing the theme of the lost fortifications. This time, the houses are interspersed with 1930s 'Tudorbethan' designs. Gardens of this era also had their own distinctive elements such as crazy paving, birdbaths, low brick walls and ornamental ponds.
(February 2002)

A typical porchway in decorative brickwork and a front door that meant home to anyone born between 1930 and 1960. The house has its name spelt out in ornamental stained glass. Most importantly, the windows carry the design that epitomised everything about the Art Deco style, the sunburst. In the 1950s, front gates were of solid wood in the sunburst design but were superseded by plainer, less symbolic designs in wrought iron. (February 2002)

Not everything in Hilsea was unpainted brickwork. Doyle Court, here photographed by Garrick Palmer, was constructed in the horizontal International Style. The buildings give the illusion of just consisting of a single wall with nothing substantial behind them – this impression of weightlessness is the fundamental visual test of whether a building is 1930s or later. (February 2002)

47

The Southdown Bus Garage

Construction of the Southdown Bus Garage by Roy Corke Building Contractors on the east side of the London Road. It opened in 1934 and was to become a familiar landmark in Hilsea and an important coach stop. (October 1933) COURTESY OF PORTSMOUTH CITY MUSEUM & RECORDS SERVICE

The construction site looking south–north with Portsdown Hill in the distance. The posts of Portsbridge can just be seen in the centre. (October 1933) COURTESY OF PORTSMOUTH CITY MUSEUM & RECORDS SERVICE

The completed facade with a lay-by in front for the coaches. This was the first major building seen by any traveller entering Portsea Island and was a fine example of the 1930s' Art Deco style of architecture – the very latest fashion in 1934. The architect is probably a relative of A.E. Cogswell. Today, the garage has become the Depot of the Southern Co-Operative Dairies Ltd., but the Art Deco design is largely unchanged. The border design around the main door, which appears to run up and down simultaneously, is still intact. (1934)
COURTESY OF PORTSMOUTH CITY MUSEUM & RECORDS SERVICE

The completed garage from the other side of the London Road with an old-style telegraph pole outside. The lamp-post on the right is a design typical in Portsmouth at the time and the wires in the centre are for the trolley buses. (1934)
COURTESY OF PORTSMOUTH CITY MUSEUM & RECORDS SERVICE

The interior of the bus garage with the coaches lined up against the wall. (1934)
COURTESY OF PORTSMOUTH CITY MUSEUM & RECORDS SERVICE

More building work was also going on just over the water. Portsbridge Boosting Station, constructed by the Portsmouth Water Company and designed by Arthur Cogswell, came into use in August 1929. It was needed in response to building development in the northern part of Portsea Island in the 1920s, and the subsequent increased demand for water; pressure would fall in Southsea because the northern part of the city could draw on supplies first. The boosting station's electric pumps would boost the pressure in the mains during periods of peak demand. Again, it was a distinctive landmark to anyone travelling down the old A3 into Portsmouth. (September 1929)
COURTESY OF PORTSMOUTH WATER

These giant frames were known as the cages and were situated either side of Portscreek – the boosting station can be seen in the background. Their purpose was to protect the access to the large shafts which led to the tunnel running under Portscreek. This tunnel contained four 36-inch pipes which supplied the City of Portsmouth with water. (May 1935)
COURTESY OF PORTSMOUTH WATER

In 1936 the public open space just the other side of Portsbridge was renamed the George V Playing Field in memory of King George V who had died in January. This plaque, showing the Lion of England in relief, stands at the gate. (February 2002)

The Unicorn of England in relief guards the other side. (February 2002)

A postcard, dating from the 1930s, showing Portsbridge where the cage on the Hilsea side can just be made out behind the lorry crossing the bridge going towards Cosham.

A very early postcard of the Hilsea Bastion Gardens dated about 1934 and seen from the top of the terraces. The swimming pool complex and the footbridge over the moat have yet to be built but on the right, a small platform can be seen which was used by the band when they played for open-air dancing. The Southdown Bus Garage can be seen in the distance.

A postcard dating from the early 1930s shows three people on a bench, one lady is wearing a stylish cloche hat with a flower in it, calmly surveying the vista of the new gardens at Hilsea with Portsbridge in the background. The putting green has just been laid out but the banks of the moat have yet to be made up to form the boating lake.

THE BOOK OF HILSEA

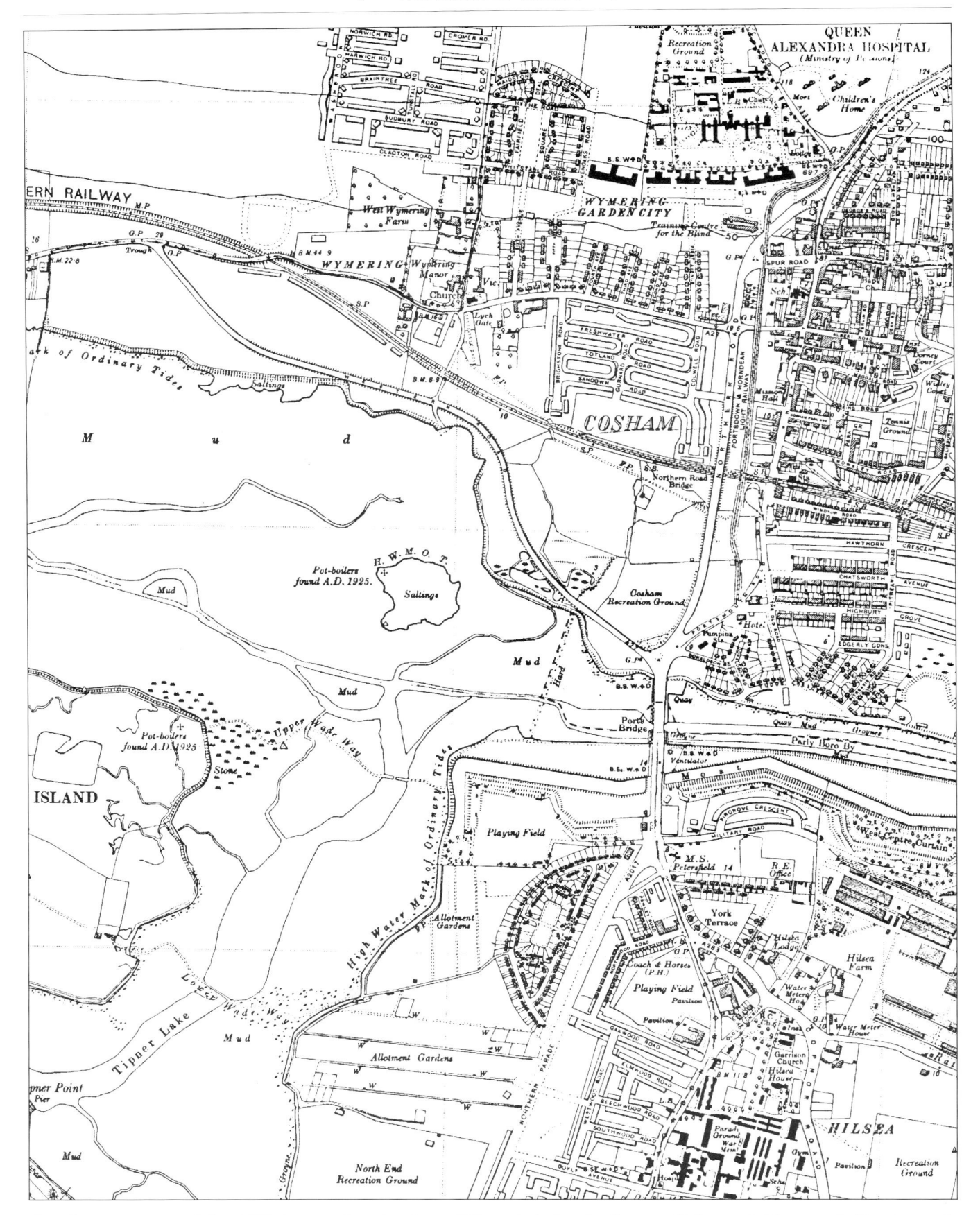

Another segment of the 1930s' map showing how Hilsea is being built up. Oakwood, Elmwood, Beechwood, Southwood, Westwood and Northwood Roads have appeared and link Northern Parade to the London Road. The old rural part of Hilsea is slowly being surrounded by building development and the three ponds seem to have disappeared from view.

The City of Portsmouth Boys' School stands adjacent to Oakwood Road. Originally Hilsea College it was taken over by the navy during the Second World War. (November 2001)

A road and railway map of the late 1930s illustrates the transport links to Portsea Island which are quite different from those of Hayling Island and Selsey Bill. Portsbridge is still the only road on to Portsea Island.

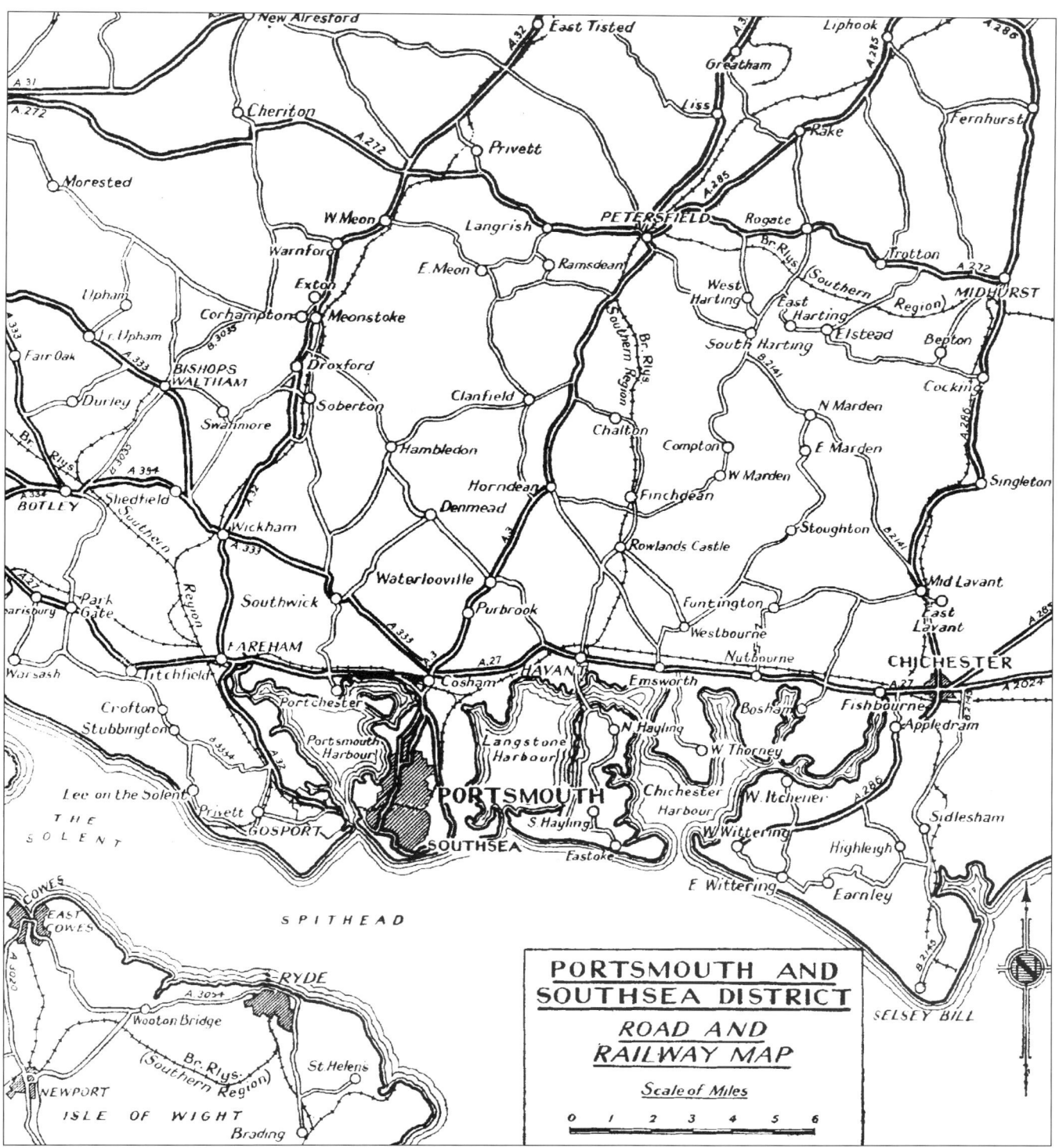

A very rare postcard, precise date unknown, of the Bastion Tea Lawns which was one of the first facilities to be opened when the Hilsea Lido site was being developed in the early 1930s. They were situated on the site of the former Hilsea Bastion which had been demolished along with the Hilsea Arches in 1919. The new terraces can just be seen in the background but the swimming pool complex has yet to be built. The steps in the centre still exist and are now behind the Bus Depot.
COURTESY OF JOHN BOWRING

A segment of the 1937 street map showing the layout of the Lido site in the far north-west corner of Portsea Island. Neither the footbridge over the moat, nor the entrance arch and tower, had yet been built but the geometric design of the public gardens is clearly visible. Designs like this were very popular at this time. This map also shows the miniature motor racing track which soon replaced the Bastion Tea Lawns. However, I have yet to see a photograph of the motor track! COURTESY OF PORTSMOUTH CITY COUNCIL

The making of the Hilsea that we know today was essentially the work of one man, Joseph Parkin, OBE, MICE. He took up the post of Deputy City Engineer to Portsmouth City Council in 1927 and in 1934 became the City Engineer. In the nineteen years until his retirement in 1953 he was responsible for many of the improvements in the north of the city, for example the completion of the Eastern Road across Portscreek, the laying out of 20 miles of private streets and the design of the original Portsbridge roundabout.

His largest single leisure project was the Hilsea Lido site which was also, apart from Southsea seafront, the largest leisure project that Portsmouth has ever known, either before or since. Consisting of about 10 acres it was developed over ten years as a 1930s' pleasure park.
(July 1938)
COURTESY THE NEWS

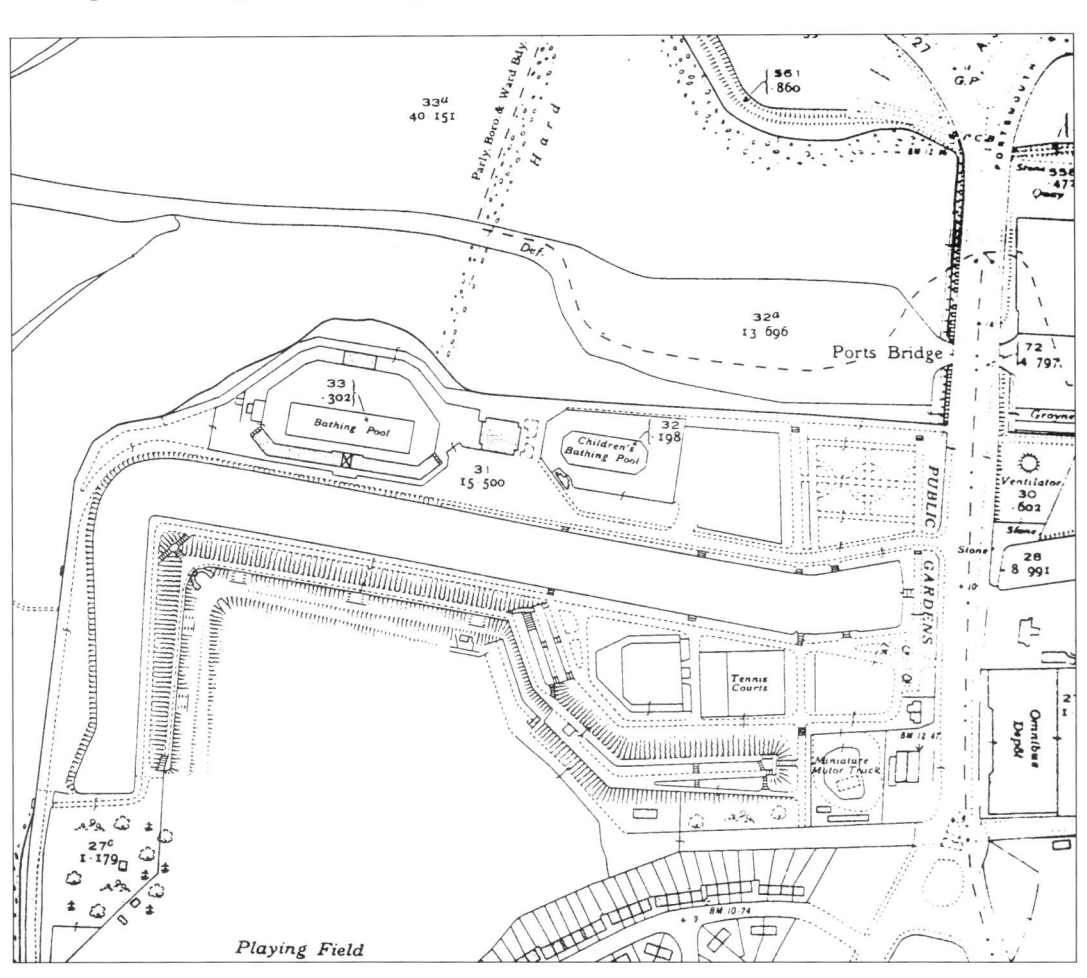

Chapter 7 1929–1939
HILSEA LIDO:
THE PLEASURE PARK IN THE NORTH

*I have wonderful memories of Hilsea Lido, I was there the day it opened,
we all thought it was the greatest thing that could happen.
There was the high diving board, water carnivals,
and a man with only one leg set himself alight and dived in...*

Mrs Joyce Arnett, local resident, in a letter to The News, 14 August 1995.

An architectural phenomenon of the 1930s, the lido combined stylish and sophisticated design with the political and social aims of the massive reconstruction which followed the First World War. The term originally derived from the Italian word *litus*, meaning shore; in particular the chain of sandy islets which separates the lagoon of Venice from the Adriatic Sea and which had developed as a luxury holiday resort for the rich. The meaning gradually expanded to include the notion of a bathing beach or open-air swimming pool, even a pleasure resort, usually beside the sea. Eventually, the concept of a luxurious resort and open-air pool become synonymous with the word lido.

In addition, outdoor activities had become a major influence in the growth of modern architecture. The stylish characteristics of modernism, white surfaces, expansive glazing and flat roofs for sunbathing had become symbolic of the cult of sunlight. The lido, especially, came to represent the streamlined stylishness of the great ocean liners with its long, long lines, pastel colours and nautical features.

Many lidos were built around the country in the 1930s, including in their amenities shingle beaches, sunbathing and spectator terraces, flower beds, cascades, water chutes and diving boards, as well as cafés. Towels and bathing costumes could be hired and water carnivals, diving exhibitions and swimming competitions of various kinds were held.

As to their design, most lidos were municipal developments for local people and usually designed by borough engineers or local architects in a great variety of styles, often very imaginatively. In some places situated on inhospitable terrain, lidos were designed to overcome the problems of rocks, dangerous currents or shallow water at low tide. Seaside pools offered the health-giving properties of sea water and an alternative to fresh water but in a more controlled manner than the sea by means of tidal filling or pumped and filtered sea-water. In the 1930s, few ordinary people could afford to go abroad for their holidays, so the new lidos and their architecture brought a hint of the luxury of the ocean liner to their surroundings, and the romance and sophistication of the 1930s to their lives.

The basic design of the urban lido was a simple square compound with rectangular baths, large enough for galas and competitions, surrounded by brick walls with buildings placed at intervals along them. The principal feature was a cascade shaped like a tiered wedding cake placed at one end. The cascade was the aerator which ensured the continual movement of the water while an engine house at one end constantly pumped clean water through the bath. The seaside lidos, however, were usually located as near to the sea as possible and often designed in imaginative, irregular shapes in response to the local landscape. This was possible because they were not constrained by the needs of competitive swimming which dominated inland pools.

Hilsea has the characteristics of both types of lido: the basic, functional design of the rectangular adult pool, large enough to allow swimming competitions and high diving, cascades, and originally, flower beds and plenty of space for sunbathing and physical recreation.

It was also designed to make optimum use of the dual problem of a large, unwieldy-shaped site and an unsafe piece of foreshore known as the Saltings, which local children had previously used for bathing. It also transformed a previously undeveloped area, which was described as a 'dirty corner of Hilsea' into 'a very beautiful place'. In 1935, Hilsea Lido was a source of great pride and 'a fine city achievement'.

The Construction of the Swimming Bath Complex 1934–1935

The boating pool is already proving popular – note the swan-shaped boats. Date of photograph: 21 May 1934.
COURTESY OF THE NEWS

Another very early and rare view of the boating lake, date unknown, this time shown from further down the moat. The top half of the lake has a barrier across it, presumably to stop the small children from going any further. The swan-shaped boats did not reappear after the war.

The site of the swimming bath complex as work starts on its construction. (June 1934)
COURTESY OF THE NEWS

The construction of the changing accommodation. (March 1935)
COURTESY OF THE NEWS

The concrete lining of the main pool. (April 1935)
COURTESY OF THE NEWS

The diving tower is added next. (July 1935) COURTESY OF THE NEWS

The children's pool is nearly finished. Note the clear view of the cascade which was demolished in the 1960s. (June 1935)
COURTESY OF THE NEWS

The construction of the road leading to the swimming bath complex. The terraces and moat can be seen in the background. (September 1934)
COURTESY OF THE NEWS

Work begins on Stamshaw Esplanade which will provide the people of Hilsea with a continuous seafront from Alexandra Park to Hilsea Lido. (September 1936)
COURTESY OF THE NEWS

Right: The sides of the moat are being built up to provide for the boating lake. (March 1937) COURTESY OF THE NEWS

Below right: The new esplanade is complete. Note that it is called Hilsea Esplanade here but is marked as Stamshaw Esplanade on many maps. (September 1938) COURTESY OF THE NEWS

An esplanade was constructed between the swimming bath complex and Portscreek in order to provide a sea wall. Nowadays, this esplanade still exists but was obscured when the motorway was built in the 1970s. (July 1935) COURTESY OF THE NEWS

A view of the new Stamshaw Esplanade. The tide is out in Tipner Lake. (November 1937) COURTESY OF THE NEWS

The Opening of the Main Pool, 24 July 1935

The first photograph of the new swimming pool which shows the opening ceremony and appeared in *The News* later on that day. (July 1935) COURTESY OF THE NEWS

A selection of views taken on the opening day which appeared in *The News* the following day. (July 1935) COURTESY OF THE NEWS

CITY OF PORTSMOUTH
HILSEA SWIMMING POOL
THIS POOL
WAS OPENED BY
THE RIGHT WORSHIPFUL
THE LORD MAYOR
COUNCILLOR FRANK J. PRIVETT J.P.
ON 24TH JULY 1935.

PIERS, BEACH, AND PUBLICITY COMMITTEE

| ALDERMAN A. BOSWORTH WRIGHT, J.P. | | CHAIRMAN |
| COUNCILLOR WALLACE S. R. PUGSLEY | | VICE-CHAIRMAN |

ALDERMEN

| W. A. BILLING O.B.E. J.P. | G. W. CORBIN J.P. | J. E. SMITH J.P. |

COUNCILLORS

F. J. SPICKERNELL	D. L. DALEY	LL. LLOYD EVANS
J. H. PRINCE	F. BEDDOW D.Sc. J.P.	A. G. STAPLEFORD
J. LIPPIETT	G. M. O'RORKE C.I.E. M.B.E.	J. J. MAHONEY
H. LAY	Mrs L. J. RAMSDEN	R. N. HICKSON
J. A. GRIFFITHS J.P.	A. J. PEARSON	E. FOOKES

F. J. SPARKS — TOWN CLERK
JOSEPH PARKIN Assoc M Inst C.E. — CITY ENGINEER
MESSRS. BOLTON & LAKIN — CONTRACTORS

A photograph of the brass plaque which was unveiled at the opening ceremony and was originally sited on the wall of the spectator stand on the north side of the main pool. It was taken down when the pool was refurbished in the 1960s and never replaced. Unseen for thirty years, it was then included in the exhibition to commemorate the lido's 60th anniversary at the Norrish Central Library (Portsmouth) and then placed in the care of the City Museum. (June 1994) COURTESY OF PORTSMOUTH CITY COUNCIL

A postcard of unknown date showing the boating lake with the newly-completed swimming bath complex in the distance. The footbridge has not yet been built and the curving vista on the right along to the main pool would not be possible now as this part of the moat was filled in when the London Road was widened in the 1970s.

Hilsea Lido's Pre-War Summer 1935–1939

The first postcard of the main pool to be produced, showing it in its first season.

The matching photograph of the children's pool in its first season. This is a very rare postcard showing the rear of the cascade with its lion's spout.

A very early photograph of local people at the main pool in its opening season. The late Esther Mulliger, who was present on the opening day, poses here with two friends; the diving tower is in the background.

The adult swimming pool shown from the north side and probably in its opening season of 1935 judging by the bunting and the fashionable outfits.

The Opening of the Main Pool, 24 July 1935

The boats arriving for the boating lake at the beginning of the season. (April 1935) COURTESY OF THE NEWS

Summer 1936

Great Times at Hilsea Lido!

The first shot of the new pool at the height of its popularity. (August 1935)
COURTESY OF THE NEWS

The local Dancing their Way to Health League go through their routine at the main pool. (July 1936) COURTESY OF THE NEWS

The main pool shown when the national Olympic swimmers squad visited Hilsea. (June 1936) COURTESY OF THE NEWS

Visiting American midshipmen photographed at the main pool. (June 1936)
COURTESY OF THE NEWS

Gala Fun at the Lido!

Novelty events at the main pool were highly popular. (August 1936)
COURTESY OF THE NEWS

Above right: The entrance of the carnival queen for the aquatic gala. (August 1936)
COURTESY OF THE NEWS

Right: One of the first shots of the children's pool which was always extremely popular. (August 1936)
COURTESY OF THE NEWS

More sporting events in the 1936 season. (August 1936)
COURTESY OF THE NEWS

The Lido in Winter 1937

Summer 1937

In the winter the open-air dancing rink was used for roller-skating and hockey. (January 1937) COURTESY OF THE NEWS

Swimming lessons were available at the main pool. (May 1937) COURTESY OF THE NEWS

PA selection of photographs of events at the main pool. (September 1937) COURTESY OF THE NEWS

The magnificent Dupree Cup was won by Mr. F. J. Magee. It is being presented by Mrs. V. Blanchard, wife of the Captain.

Hilsea Lido on Saturday afternoon. Most of the spectators were glad of overcoats and mackintoshes.

Centre: Start of the final of the North End Business Men's Association Cup. Miss Gubby, second from the left was the winner.

Miss Zetta Hill demonstrates her special water cycle at the main pool.

67

> **HILSEA SWIMMING POOL**
> TO-NIGHT AND THURSDAY.
> EACH EVENING AT 8.15 P.M.
> WONDERFUL ATTRACTION!!
> AN EPIC OF THE WAR.
> **THE BLOCKING OF ZEEBRUGGE**
> A MINIATURE REPRODUCTION
> OF THIS
> THRILLING SPECTACLE.
> WITH 70 MODEL SHIPS, SEARCHLIGHTS, SHELL FIRE, BLOWING UP OF THE VIADUCT BY SUBMARINE C.3, ETC.
> YOU SHOULD NOT MISS
> THIS GREAT DISPLAY.
> ADMISSION 1/- and 6d. Inc. Tax.

> **HILSEA SWIMMING POOL**
> SATURDAY AT 3 p.m.
> *Great Attraction!!*
> **AQUATIC GALA**
> INCLUDING
> DIVING CHAMPIONSHIPS
> OF HAMPSHIRE.
> 1 MEN'S, 2 WOMEN'S, 3, GIRLS'.
> 'WOOLGAR' SWIMMING
> CHALLENGE CUP.
> RELAY RACES.
> PORTSMOUTH SCHOOLS' TEAM
> CHAMPIONSHIPS
> **POLO MATCH.**
> NORTHSEA S.C. (Portsmouth) v.
> PIRELLI GENERAL S.C. (Southampton).
> SOME OF THE FINEST DIVERS
> IN THE COUNTY WILL
> PARTICIPATE
> ADMISSION ... ... 6d.

An advertisement for a re-enactment by model ships of the First World War Naval Battle. (September 1937)
COURTESY OF THE NEWS

Events at the lido were widely publicised. Here is an advertisement for an aquatic gala in the 1937 season. (September 1937)
COURTESY OF THE NEWS

> OPENING FRIDAY, 3rd JUNE
> **HILSEA SWIMMING POOL**
> PORTSBRIDGE
> Buses "A" and "B" and Trolley Buses 2, 3 & 4, take you there.
> CAFE ——— TEA LAWNS
> Adults 6d., Juniors 3d., Spectators 2d.
> Swimming and Diving Lessons 6d.
> LARGE CAR PARK FREE.

An advertisement for the new summer season showing admission charges, travel directions, free car parking and now, swimming and diving lessons. (May 1938) COURTESY OF THE NEWS

An advertisement for an aquatic gala in the 1938 season. (July 1938)
COURTESY OF THE NEWS

> **HILSEA SWIMMING POOL**
> SATURDAY AT 3 P.M.
> **GRAND AQUATIC GALA**
> INCLUDING
> MEN'S DIVING CHAMPIONSHIP
> OF ENGLAND.
> EXHIBITIONS, TEAM RACE,
> POLO MATCH.
> AN AFTERNOON OF
> SPORT.
> ADMISSION - - - 6d.

Summer 1938

The presentation of an award for a competitive swimming event. (July 1938)
COURTESY OF THE NEWS

Competitive diving was considered great sport at Hilsea and attracted many spectators. (July 1938) COURTESY OF THE NEWS

The hottest day of the year! This picture taken on 2 August 1938 would be one much repeated in years to come. COURTESY OF THE NEWS

The children's water chute at the west end of the bath. (September 1938) COURTESY OF THE NEWS

A very unusual shot of the boating lake with the landing stage, hut and gardens in the background by the tennis courts. (April 1939) COURTESY OF THE NEWS

Bridging Hilsea Lido

The footbridge over the moat was constructed between March and August 1938 in order to give better access to the swimming bath complex from the rest of the site. Here, work is shown just commencing. The bridge was demolished in 1999 and at the time of writing is due to be replaced. (March 1938)
COURTESY OF THE NEWS

The new bridge nears completion. (May 1938)
COURTESY OF THE NEWS

August 1938 and the bridge is completed. It was considered to be very picturesque and attractive by local people. (August 1938)
COURTESY OF THE NEWS

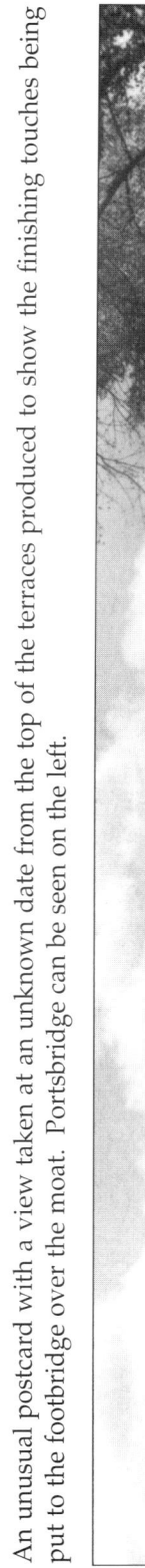

An unusual postcard with a view taken at an unknown date from the top of the terraces produced to show the finishing touches being put to the footbridge over the moat. Portsbridge can be seen on the left.

The Hilsea Bastion Gardens

A photograph from the local paper showing the new gardens with their unusual geometric design which had just been created on the Hilsea Lido site next to the London Road. The Bastion Road House has not yet been rebuilt and the Southdown Bus Garage can be seen on the right. (September 1936) COURTESY OF THE NEWS

Much time and effort was spent in landscaping the whole lido site as shown in this view of the newly-laid out gardens overlooking the boating lake. (September 1937)
COURTESY OF THE NEWS

A view of the new gardens looking east–west towards the children's paddling pool. (October 1938)
COURTESY OF THE NEWS

An undated view from the top of the terraces, unusually in vertical form, showing the bridge just about to be completed. The swimming bath complex stands uncluttered and free from undergrowth.

A more detailed shot, again undated, showing the decorative brickwork on the terraces and the new bridge. The terraces were demolished in 2000.

An undated postcard with a picturesque shot of the pergola, roses and terrace of the Hilsea pleasure gardens which was a very popular spot for courting couples. The tennis courts and the putting green can be seen in the background.

The Entrance Arch and Tower

The last feature of the lido site to be constructed and the first to disappear, the entrance arch and tower was designed by Adrien Sharp, the city architect appointed in 1936. The design at the top of the tower echoed that of the tower at Lee-on-Solent and the unembellished lettering with its distinct spatial divisions was typical of the Modern Movement in architecture. The lettering is a contrast to the rather fussy Art Nouveau style letters on the South Down Bus Garage opposite. Local people could buy sweets and ice-creams in the kiosk as they arrived at the lido site.

The entrance arch and tower was a landmark at the gateway to Portsmouth for thirty years until it was demolished in 1968 when the Portsbridge roundabout was widened. However, some of the decorative lamp posts shown in the photograph still remain on the lido site. COURTESY OF PORTSMOUTH CITY MUSEUM & RECORDS SERVICE

A Last Look at the Pre-War Pool

A view taken in the 1930s showing the main pool. The plaque can just be seen on the far right on the front of the spectator stand and the shot gives a very clear impression of the pool as the deck of a huge liner. The sun-decks face out to sea with the small 'bridge' on top. Portchester Castle can be seen in the distance – a view which would be impossible today because of the M275.
COURTESY OF THE NEWS

The lido's fifth season in 1939 was its last before the Second World War. This advertisement poignantly announces the last performance of the 1939 water show, the date of the photograph is 15 July 1939. Seven weeks later, on 3 September war was declared against Germany.
COURTESY OF THE NEWS

HILSEA SWIMMING POOL
LAST PERFORMANCE.
TO-NIGHT AT 8
SATURDAY AFTERNOON AT 3.
A RIOT OF THRILLS,
COMEDY & GLAMOUR.

WATER SHOW OF 1939

WORLD CHAMPIONS PRESENT;
THE GREATEST WATER CIRCUS
EVER SEEN IN PORTSMOUTH.
VIDE PRESS:
MARVELLOUS.
Admission: 2/- and 1/-
Children: Half-price.

A Favourite Landmark – The Bastion Road House and Its Cannon

A lovely 1930s-style advertisement for the rebuilt Bastion Road House which opened in 1938 to replace the original building which had been demolished. It was built by the firm of Messrs Howe & Bishop of Clarendon Street, Portsmouth, but the identity of the architect is unknown.

The cannon pictured was one of a pair which had a most interesting history. According to correspondence in *The News* in 1956, the cannon were two of several presented to the City of Portsmouth in 1855 after the victory at Sebastopol in the Crimean War. They were then placed on Clarence Parade where they remained until the 1920s when they were removed to a corporation yard.

In 1937 they were sold to the Bastion Road House and put on display outside. For nearly twenty years they were a landmark at Portsbridge. In 1956 they were sold as part of a massive auction of café equipment and other effects when the Road House closed and became a garage. Their location is now unknown. The Bastion Road House building was demolished in the 1980s. (September 1938)
COURTESY OF THE NEWS

The official farewell ceremony in 1945 when Hilsea Barracks was handed back to the RAOC. The Americans salute the Stars and Stripes. COURTESY OF THE RLC MUSEUM

Chapter 8 1939–1945
WARTIME AND THE AMERICANS

*In about 1942 (at Hilsea Lido) I saw some black American soldiers using the boats –
one fell in and the others dived in to join him – all laughing – real comradeship.*

From a response to a questionnaire at the 60th Anniversary of Hilsea Lido Exhibition, 1995.

Hilsea was spared the devastating bomb damage that reduced the centres of Portsmouth and Southsea to rubble. There was very little destruction in Hilsea and amazingly, the very large lido site emerged unscathed. However, what Hilsea did have was the Americans. The years 1943 to 1945 saw what was described at the time as an American occupation as its troops took over Hilsea Barracks. They arrived in April 1943 to service their troops in the area and supply the D-Day Invasion Army. The Royal and Mechanical Engineers' workshops were taken over and thousands of tons of war supplies shipped out from there.

The depot was known as G65 and some 10 000 men served there. It was considered to be one of the happiest stations in the UK. Certainly, many local people have memories of the Americans giving the local children sweets and relaxing at the lido.

In 1944, the 13 units stationed there included: 235 Quartermasters Salvage Company, Detachment A; 519 Quartermasters Battalion M Headquarters and Headquarters Detachment; 604 B ARMT M Battalion; 864 Ordnance Heavy Automotive Maintenance Company; 904 Ordnance Heavy Automotive Maintenance Company; 278 Ordnance MAA Company; 283 Quartermasters REFG Company; 283 Quartermasters RFG Company; 346 Quartermasters DEP CO S; 42 FIN DISB SEC; G-65 General Depot; 120 CML PROC CO and 3691 Quartermasters TRK CO.

The American Officer in Charge, Major E.E. Mack, of the Quartermaster Corps of the US Army was awarded the Bronze Star for his work at Hilsea when in 1945 the depot was handed back to the RAOC. The Americans were dispersed around the country, some to go on to other units and some to return home. One interesting feature of the work at the depot was the construction of field caravans or trailers, such as the one used by Field Marshal Montgomery in the field. The design for the trailers was based on a model by a Mr Farley, a civilian employee. Some of the ex-soldiers have since returned to Hilsea for a nostalgic tour of their former barracks.

The Stars and Stripes being lowered.
COURTESY OF THE RLC MUSEUM

The Stars and Stripes being presented to the British Officer in Charge, Major J.G. Macfarlane, RAOC.
COURTESY OF THE RLC MUSEUM

The RAOC pennant is hoisted.
COURTESY OF THE RLC MUSEUM

The Hilsea Lido site remained open during the war but the main pool was closed to civilians. The Armed Forces stationed in Hilsea were allowed to use it and each unit was allocated a different day. Here, the RAOC parade in front of it. (c.1945) COURTESY OF THE NEWS

Hilsea railway station was constructed in 1941 and was originally known as Hilsea Halt. Several branch lines led off the main railway line to a marshalling yard and sidings for the transport of stores to the RAOC depot at the rear of the Hilsea lines. The station was originally a Bailey bridge but was re-built and still exists today although the eastern side of the depot has been replaced by an industrial site. However, the original gate which led to the branch lines can still be seen. After the war, Hilsea along with other stations in the area, dropped the title of Halt. (November 2001)

The civilian population did their bit during the war. This is a very unusual postcard showing members of the Fire Service. Sparshatt's was the main dealers for many commercial vehicles at this time and their premises can be seen in the background with the Coach and Horses pub to the right. Date of photograph unknown.
COURTESY OF JOHN BOWRING

This postcard, date unknown, shows a static water storage tank situated opposite the Ministry of Defence houses in York Terrace on the London Road. These tanks were used in wartime to store water for putting out fires in case the mains supply should be disrupted by bombing. They could be seen all over Portsmouth but were rarely photographed and disappeared immediately the war ended. COURTESY OF JOHN BOWRING

Sparshatt's again, this time manoeuvring what is probably a water container. This shot is taken at the rear of the Walberant buildings shopping parade, in Sparshatt's yard. COURTESY OF JOHN BOWRING

Chapter 9 1946–1952
LIFE RETURNS TO NORMAL

The late 1940s and early 1950s were the years of austerity. Rationing was still in force and did not end until 1951, the housing shortage was acute, consumer goods were in short supply and everyday life was still dominated by the Armed Services in that most men had either just been demobbed, were still in them or about to join them. National Service conscription was still in force, not ending until 1960.

In spite of that, ordinary families relished the thought of no more war. Couples who had postponed marriage because of the war could now marry and were pleased to have to chance to start a family and bring up children in peacetime conditions.

In Hilsea, all these new families needed houses. So in 1945, as in many other parts of the country, 53 prefabs (short for pre-fabricated) houses were erected in various parts of Northern Parade and others just over Portsbridge in Cosham. Portsmouth was allocated 1400 and although only supposed to be temporary at the time, as elsewhere, these homes lasted until the 1960s when the families who lived in them were rehoused.

On 14 December 1948, a new community centre was opened when St Francis' Youth Centre on the corner of Northern Parade was replaced by the Northern Parade Community Centre. This became the focal point for social activities for the residents of the Hilsea Crescent area until 1999.

The late 1940s were known as the post-war baby boom and it was certainly a golden time for children in spite of what might be considered as hardships today. Hilsea Lido reopened in 1947 and more facilities were on offer then than at any other time in its history. There was something for everyone, for all ages and all members of the family. The lido site was easily accessible from all parts of Portsmouth and was advertised widely by the City Council.

In addition to the adult swimming pool, the children's paddling pool and the café, there was a miniature railway which ran all the way around the site, along with a putting green, tennis courts, and the gardens and terraces. Open-air dancing was laid on for the adults and as the area was floodlit at night, there was plenty to do in the evenings as well. Many local people held their wedding receptions and twenty-first birthday parties at the function room in the café and had photographs taken on the white, oriental-style footbridge over the moat.

The adult swimming pool was open from 7am in the morning until 10pm at night and there was much more to do there than just swimming. There were two water chutes, a small one for the younger children and a higher one for older ones. There were at least three one-metre diving boards, and of course the diving tower with its high board of 32 feet (10 metres). It was the highest board in Hampshire at the time but only a few ever dared to dive from it.

The boating lake was always very popular, with a mixture of pedal boats, rowing boats and canoes for hire. A fascinating feature of the boating lake was the board showing a number of clock faces with movable hands which would indicate how long each boat had on the water. When time ran out the superintendent would shout out, 'Time's up, number 6!'

As the site was so large there was always plenty of room for all sorts of games, and the terraces and ramparts were wonderful places for children to play. The Stamshaw Esplanade with its walk around from the lido to Alexandra Park was a great favourite too, especially when the tide was out and it was possible to walk along the shingle. It made a nice end to any visit.

Life in the Barracks

This photograph shows the Remembrance Day Parade held on 8 November 1947 at Hilsea Barracks. The large war memorial, known as the Camp Cenotaph, on the east side of the parade square had been unveiled in 1922 and was dedicated to those who had lost their lives in the Great War. The memorial carried 606 names culminating in the Latin motto: SUA TELA TONANTI. Also: 'They be of Those That Have Left a Name Behind Them'. In fact, this was the last Remembrance Day Parade in front of this memorial as in the following year, it was removed to the newly established Corps Headquarters at Deepcut, Camberley. A stone plaque was left in its place. COURTESY OF THE RLC MUSEUM

The RAOC was very much a part of ordinary Hilsea life. Soldiers in uniform were a common sight in the local streets in a way that is not the case today. This shows troops returning to the barracks from church parade. The last line of the band can just be seen passing through the gate. Date of photograph: 1950–51. COURTESY OF THE RLC MUSEUM

Here, a company of the ATS (Auxiliary Territorial Service) leaves the main gate. Date of photograph: c.1950.
COURTESY OF THE RLC MUSEUM

Major Hynes, MC takes 'B' Company passing-out parade at Hilsea Barracks, c.1950. The RSM stands close by. This is a very familiar, though not always pleasant, sight to anyone who has ever served in the Armed Forces!
COURTESY OF THE RLC MUSEUM

Rugby Camp

Rugby Camp had been built just before the war in 1938. It was situated opposite Hilsea Barracks, between the Copnor Road and the railway line. This is a photograph, c.1950, of the electric plate washer at the camp.
COURTESY OF THE RLC MUSEUM

The caption on this photograph, c.1950, reads, 'This machine has just washed the new American trays'.
COURTESY OF THE RLC MUSEUM

This caption reads, 'Trainees being served lunch, Cook Private A. Moon on right'. (c.1950) COURTESY OF THE RLC MUSEUM

Ron Boyland stands outside the Bastion Road House on the other side of the London Road. This is a very rare shot, again from 1949, of one of the cannon outside.

The war might be over but here is Ron Boyland in 1949 in his RAF uniform on the footbridge over the moat with the terraces in the background.

THOS. COOK & SON LTD.
Head Office: BERKELEY ST., LONDON, W.1
with Branches everywhere
will give enquirers all information and literature relating to
SOUTHSEA and the City of PORTSMOUTH

SOUTH PARADE TEA HOUSE
(next SOUTH PARADE PIER)
has a wonderful variety of Chocolate and Confectionery in stock throughout the year
ICES · MINERALS · TEAS · CAKES
Always a good variety of Postcards, Children's Toys, Games, Buckets and Spades

When in Southsea do not forget to visit
THE HILSEA LIDO
PORTSBRIDGE, PORTSMOUTH
One of the finest Open-air Sea-water Swimming Pools in England. Delightful Children's Paddling Pool close by, also the Moat where Boats are available. The **Miniature Railway** is a great attraction, the track being over half-a-mile in length
Lovely GARDENS · CAFE · CAR PARK

When Hilsea Lido opened again post-war, it was advertised in the City Council's tourist guide book in 1947 as a great attraction. People began to take summer holidays again and even holiday-makers staying in Southsea were encouraged to visit. Features were now to be geared more to families with children as opposed to sporting events and included a café and a miniature railway.
(1946) COURTESY OF PORTSMOUTH CITY COUNCIL

Sport had also resumed at Alexandra Park. Here is a c.1940s view of a cycle race with the new pavilion in the background.
COURTESY OF THE HAMPSHIRE TELEGRAPH

The Hilsea Tenants' Association 1946–1951

The Association was organised for the benefit of the residents of the Hilsea Crescent area in the years following the war and was very active in issues concerning rent increases. Here members are shown in 1949 taking part in a demonstration in response to a proposed rent rise. Elsie Craigie is shown on the far left.

The austere conditions of life in the 1940s with rationing still in force did not stop people from enjoying themselves, as in this 1949 shot. A very important social event for the Hilsea Tenants' Association was the weekly dance held at St Saviour's Hall in Twyford Avenue.

The Tenants' Association also organised many social functions. Here, a group of residents are waiting to board Byng's Coaches to go on an outing to Basset in Southampton in the 1940s. A little girl on the left has the slogan, 'Have a Go Joe' on her bonnet. This was all the rage at the time and perhaps came from the American troops based at Hilsea Barracks. Elsie Craigie is second from right.

A second shot of the Hilsea families' outing to Southampton.

The Prefabs and Family Life

The first prefabs in Portsmouth were constructed in Hilsea off Northern Parade and Cosham had a group just across Portsbridge. As in Hilsea Crescent, the people who lived in them formed a large, closely knit community. This was the time of the post-war baby boom and there were children everywhere. This was a wonderful time for local children; the prefabs all had large gardens for them to play in, there was the lido, the George V playing field, the Cosham Bowling Green and Portsbridge, which was a pleasant walk across Portscreek. COURTESY OF THE HAMPSHIRE TELEGRAPH

It was a sad day in 1964 when the prefabs were pulled down and the families had to move to Southampton Road in Cosham where they were rehoused. The Cosham site is now occupied by Lynx House, the building used by the Inland Revenue. (1947)

Mrs Haines standing in the front garden of her home in Newport Road in this c.1950 photo. This was part of the estate in central Cosham which was known as the Isle of Wight Estate as all its roads were named after places on the island. The prefabs, however, occupied a triangle of land between Western Road and Northern Road just across Portsbridge. There was Newport Road, Yarmouth Road and Portsbridge Close. This design of prefab was known as the Mark II Phoenix. The rooms were of a good size and all had front and back gardens.

Cameras were much more common now and families, especially fathers, were keen to record every stage in their children's lives in a way not seen before to such an extent. Here, a family group poses in the garden in 1948.

The girls with baby, 1948.

A nice smile! 1948.

Inside the prefab, 1948.

A group with Mum, 1948.

Just outside the front door, 1951.

THE BOOK OF HILSEA

A school group, 1950s.
Another school group, 1950s.

Eileen and Mrs Haines in the garden. A shot which gives a very good view of the front of the prefab, taken in the 1960s.

A shot of a neighbour's car in the 1950s – a very unusual sight in those days!

Northern Parade continued to be built up after the war and these houses were constructed by the Rotary Club. The plaque on the outside reads, '1938–1948: These two houses are a goodwill gift from the Rotary Club of Portsmouth and Southsea in association with the Inner Wheel'. (February 2002)

Queen Elizabeth II came to the throne following the death of George VI on 6 February 1952, her coronation taking place the following year on 2 June 1953. This was a time of great optimism, hope and relief that the hard times of the war years were at long last over, and a good opportunity to organise parties and entertainments for the children. This is the second photograph of the street party organised for the children of Horsea Road which can be seen clearly in the distance.

The children of the prefabs dressed in fancy-dress outfits on Coronation Day – a scarecrow, a boxer, a cowboy, a nurse, Little Red Riding Hood and another cowboy!

Chapter 10 **1953–1968**

A CORONATION AND A NEW LOOK TO OLD PLEASURES

The coronation of Queen Elizabeth II was a great event in 1953. Somehow, it seemed to make the war and all its privations and struggle a thing of the past. The City Council supported all types of events to celebrate it and street parties were very popular.

The 'baby-boomers' were growing up and had become or were about to become teenagers, the new phenomenon of the 1950s. Work was plentiful, the school-leaving age was 15 and for the first time, young people could have an income of their own. There was more choice in consumer goods and families gradually acquired cars, televisions, telephones and refrigerators.

By the 1960s though, change was on its way. National Service ended in 1962 and Hilsea Barracks went the way of the other Hilsea fortifications. It was closed, eventually demolished and housing built on the site. By 1968, plans had been made to widen the London Road, extend the Portsbridge roundabout and construct a motorway to link the centre of Portsmouth directly with the mainland for the first time. The lido would be more directly affected by all this than Hilsea itself, but nevertheless, things would never be the same again.

The City of Portsmouth organised many events to celebrate the coronation: a firework display, a torchlight procession and community singing on coronation night, a carnival procession and a coronation tattoo at Fratton Park. Street parties were encouraged and held between 26 May and 27 June. The best-decorated street or block of buildings was awarded a prize of £5. An official programme was produced and local shops and businesses put in special advertisements. Here's one for the Portsmouth & Brighton United Breweries Ltd, and White & Co. Ltd at North End Junction, 1953.
COURTESY PORTSMOUTH CITY COUNCIL

The prefab estate held its own coronation party, too. Every schoolchild in the country was given a commemorative coronation mug, a couple of which can be seen here on the table.

THE BOOK OF HILSEA

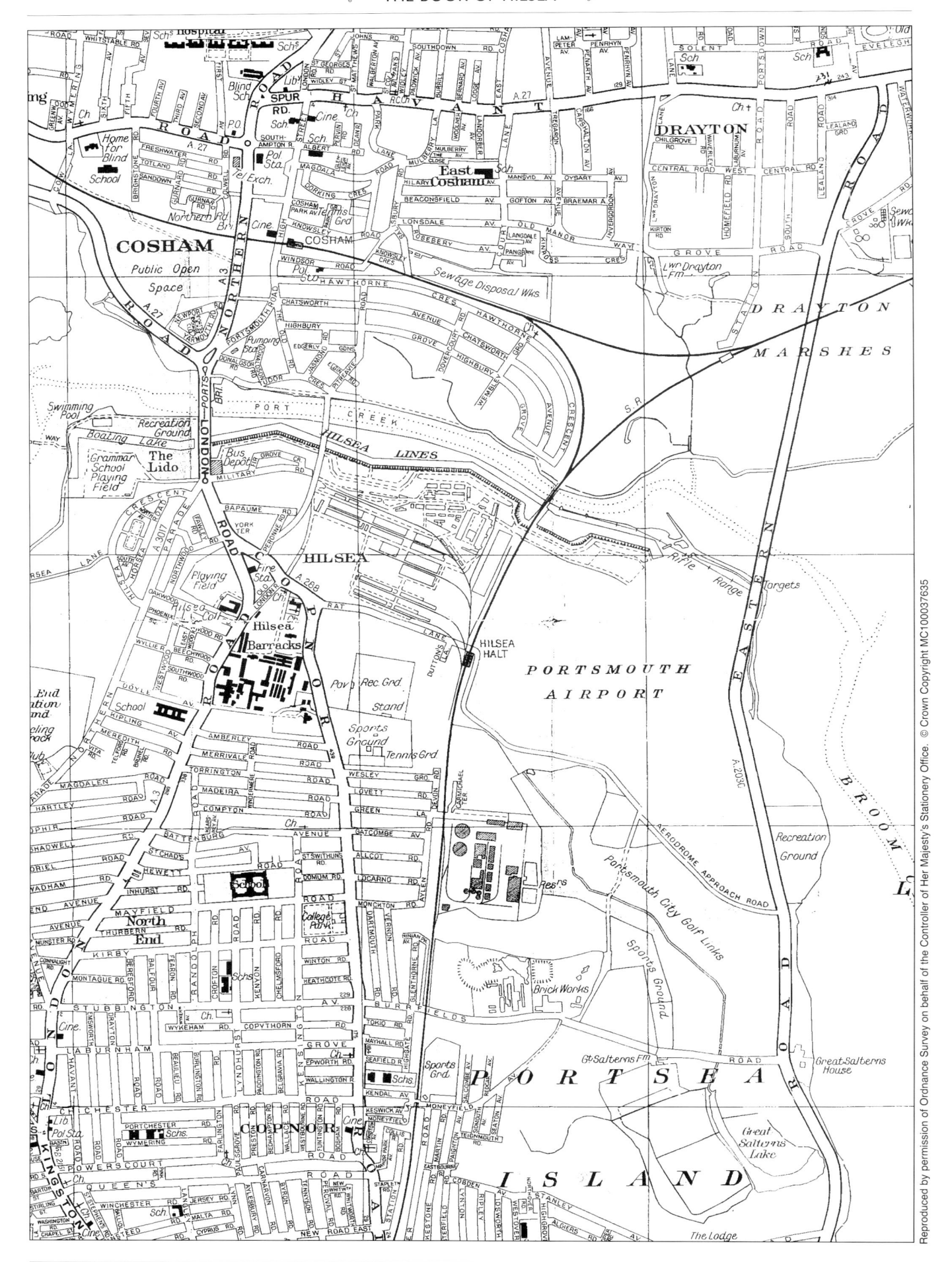

Opposite: This post-war map shows how Hilsea has changed, there is no open farmland and the small farms in the old rural centre of Hilsea are not even marked. The roads have all been built up and now reach right up to the eastern boundary along the railway line, the branch lines from Hilsea Station are shown very clearly, and the sidings have the typical layout of an RAOC stores depot. Most importantly, the Eastern Road appears for the first time and Portsbridge is no longer the only route on to Portsea Island.

Post-War Building

This vista of Northern Parade in the 1980s, by Garrick Palmer, shows the new rows of flats which had eventually replaced the prefabs.

In 1941 the First Church of Christ, Scientist, seen here in the 1950s, moved to 178 London Road from Southsea. This had formerly been the site of a very large house and they built their Reading Room there in 1954. A new church was then constructed next door and the first service was held on 26 August 1956. The church has continued to be a familiar fixture of the London Road ever since. The building was completed in 1973 with the addition of the Sunday school.

The First Church of Christ, Scientist, seen in the 1950s from the west side of the London Road.

The inside of the First Church of Christ, Scientist. (1950s)

A Favourite Park

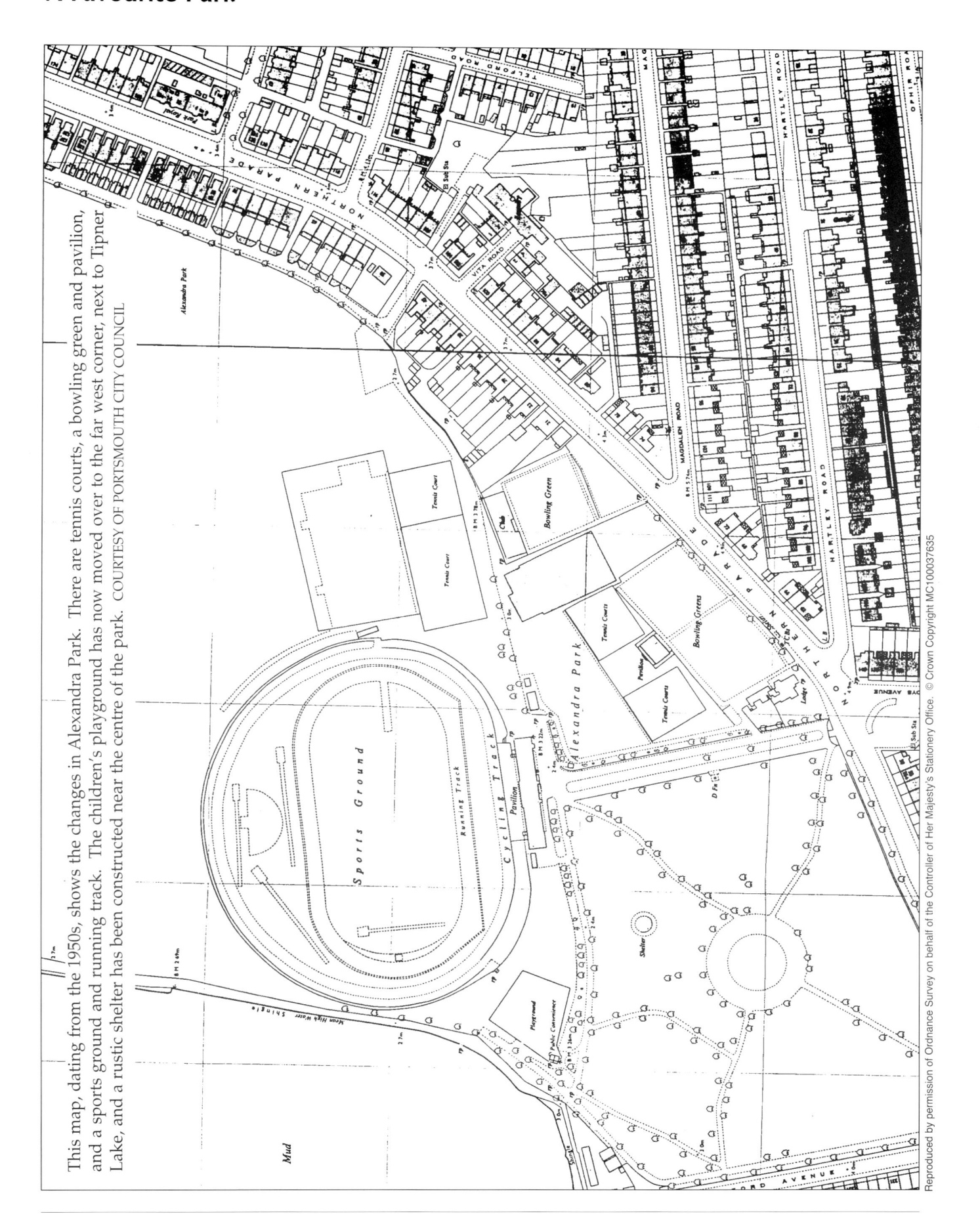

This map, dating from the 1950s, shows the changes in Alexandra Park. There are tennis courts, a bowling green and pavilion, and a sports ground and running track. The children's playground has now moved over to the far west corner, next to Tipner Lake, and a rustic shelter has been constructed near the centre of the park. COURTESY OF PORTSMOUTH CITY COUNCIL

A view, looking west–east across the park shows my sister and me on the swings in the children's playground with my mother, Bessie Constance Stark, watching in the background. A glimpse can just be had on the far left of the rustic shelter which had a thatched roof and was known as the 'monkey house'. It disappeared probably when the Mountbatten Centre was built in the 1980s. (August 1956) COURTESY OF HARRY LEONARD STARK

My sister, Lesley Stark on the roundabout known as 'the spider'. This was made of cast iron and was very heavy. The rut in the ground underneath was made by children standing in the iron 'web' and pushing it round, getting faster and faster as they went and then jumping up quickly on to the strands while it whizzed round. This provided a jolly good ride but took ages to slow down. There were also swingboats in the playground and another heavy circular roundabout but I have never seen photographs of these. Obviously not the sort of thing that children would be expected to want these days! (August 1956) COURTESY OF HARRY LEONARD STARK

The Southdown Bus Garage

The bus garage had become a very well-known landmark at the gateway to Portsmouth by the 1950s. A refreshment stall was now provided for travellers inside but did not last all that long, probably because they were enveloped in exhaust fumes as soon as the buses started their engines! The little trolley on the left in this 1950s' shot was for collecting the empties and the tables and chairs can be seen on the right.
COURTESY OF ALAN LAMBERT

The pre-war motor-racing track had long disappeared and a new bus depot was constructed on the west side of the London Road in 1954/5. This photograph shows the building in its early stages. The path in the foreground runs along to the Portsmouth Grammar School playing fields. COURTESY OF ALAN LAMBERT

Another shot of the new bus depot, this time from the back, taken from the top of the remaining ramparts. The garage in front alongside the London Road can be made out and the Southdown Bus Garage in the far top-left corner. COURTESY OF ALAN LAMBERT

The Bastion Road House

Next door to the Southdown Bus Garage, the Bastion Road House had closed in 1956, and been turned into a garage which was known as the Bastion Filling Station. There was also another filling station opposite, on the west side of the London Road. This shot was taken the following year, on 29 August 1957, and gives a good view of the 1950s' petrol pumps and the cashier's box. In those days, there was no such thing as self-service and an attendant would come out to fill up the tank. Despite the conversion, the original fancy brickwork of the Road House is quite visible, along with the ornamental window. Eventually, these were covered up. The posts in the right-hand corner belong to the lay-by of the Southdown Bus Garage and are still in existence, although without their white paint and decorative chains. The lady going by wears a fashionable 1950s' full-skirted coat, a neat little hat, smart shoes and gloves and carries a handbag. COURTESY OF ALAN LAMBERT

The 1950s and the Hey-Day of Hilsea Lido

The boating lake was always well used. The swan-shaped boats have disappeared now though in this 1950s' shot, and only rowing boats and canoes are available. COURTESY OF J.A. HEWES

The main feature of the post-war lido was the miniature railway which lasted from 1946–1951. This ran from the main pool round to the end of the moat near the London Road. The picture shows the 'station' and the footbridge over the moat in the background. A highly popular attraction, it was uneconomic and closed after five years.

This boat seems overloaded! The lovely weeping willow trees are a feature of the lido site, here in the 1950s. COURTESY OF J.A. HEWES

A very unusual 1950s' view of the far east end of the moat with the entrance arch and tower in the background. This part of the moat disappeared when the London Road was widened in the 1960s. COURTESY OF J.A. HEWES

The terraces and gardens were considered a great asset to the site in the 1950s, so much so that many postcards were produced of them. This one is postmarked 11 September 1953.

The children's pool and Hilsea Café are shown here, at an unknown date, with the cascade in the background. This was demolished in the 1960s and the diving tower of the main pool, which can just be seen in the background, went on 22 April 1971.

A rare shot, from the 1950s, of the south side of the main pool which brings out the long lines of the architecture reminiscent of the ocean liner lying in dock. The canopy can be seen over the entrance facing the moat, the miniature railway starts near the main entrance and most unusually, there are two roundabouts set up in the car park. The entrance facing the moat was unused and blocked up many years ago and the canopy demolished in the summer of 1994.

Local people pose for their picture to be taken in the 1950s.

A 1950s' view west–east across the main pool showing the small spectator stand on the north side and the chain-link fencing which separated the swimmers from the sunbathers.

Another 1950s' view of water chutes at each end of the main pool which were always popular; the one at the far end being for small children and the near one for adults and bigger children. They disappeared in the 1970s.

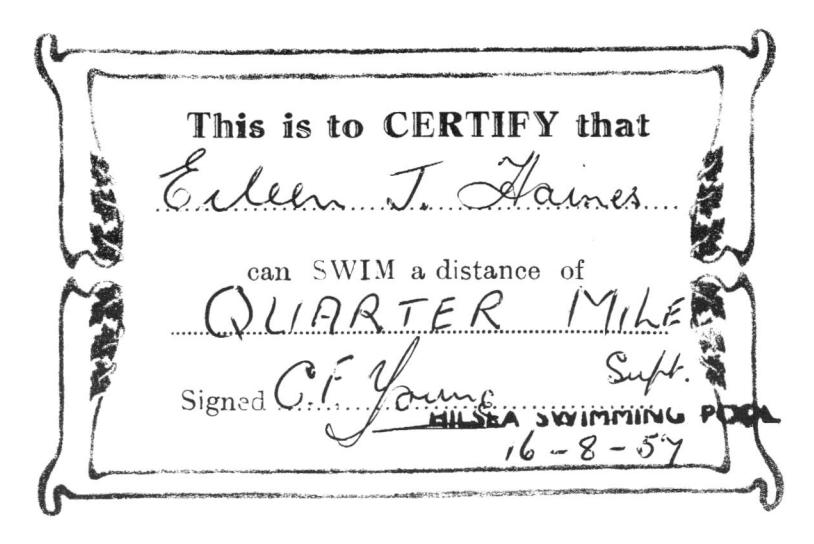

> This is to CERTIFY that Eileen J. Haines can SWIM a distance of QUARTER MILE
> Signed C.F. Young Supt.
> HILSEA SWIMMING POOL
> 16-8-57

Swimming lessons continued after the war, given by the swimming pool superintendent and instructor Mr Young who was a well-known local personality. Successful children were awarded certificates to show that they could swim certain lengths, in this case, a quarter of a mile. A length of the main pool was 220 feet so a quarter of a mile was six lengths – quite an achievement for a nine-year-old! A sad note to the history of the lido; the first fatality occurred when a young boy drowned in the main pool on 1 July 1955. (August 1957)

Events in Family Life in Oakwood Road

Christmas was still a great event for the children in the 1940s and '50s and though there was little money about just after the war, there was always a Christmas tree, decorations and mistletoe. (1950s)

A closer view of the dolls and toys decorating the tree.

A quiet moment. (1950s)

The adults always enjoyed themselves, too, with a good spread on the table – Christmas cakes, blancmanges, trifles, jelly and custard, fancy cakes on decorative stands and crackers. (1950s)

A 1950s' birthday party in the garden. This gives a good view of a glass veranda typical of many houses in Hilsea and Portsmouth. There was no such thing as a conservatory in those days, it was 'the room in the garden', but many houses had them. My grandmother always referred to hers as 'the glass house' and kept odds and ends in it.

As well as Christmas we all had birthday parties. This one is in the garden with a lovely iced cake. (1950s)

The hair bows were the latest fashion for little girls and the tricycle in the background the latest thing for the boys. (1950s)

Younger children had their fashions, too, such as this lacy sun bonnet. (1950s)

The children's party was a great feature of the 1950s. This shot includes the children's entertainer in the centre, 'Uncle Charlie', perhaps? The sticking plaster over the spectacle lens of the little boy sitting on the floor in the right foreground was a common sight in those days. The National Health Service had begun in 1948 and for the first time children could expect free health care.

The 1960s

The fifties had ended and the post-war baby boomers were becoming the first teenagers but still took part in a variety of children's activities. Here, the local Sunday school stage the traditional nativity play.

The Northern Parade Boys' School are photographed in their costumes after putting on their school play.

The Portsmouth Grammar School maintains large playing fields on the south side of Hilsea Lido. Here, a rugby team poses after a match.

Mary Mullinger wearing the latest fashion in swimming costumes here in the garden with Perry the poodle. He was named after the popular American singer, Perry Como. Most families had televisions now and were very familiar with all the current entertainers. The high garden wall made of brick is very typical of Hilsea.

St Francis' Church lunch club, organised by the Good Companions Concert party. They would cook the lunch and then provide entertainment.

A pancake day lunch at the St Francis' Church lunch club.

A close-up of the Good Companions Concert Party. They entertained voluntary groups and in old people's homes for many years and were very popular. The late Esther Mullinger is on the bottom right-hand corner.

A fashionable ladies' hairdressers now occupies one of the premises at Walberant Buildings. The large static water tanks of the war seem a long time ago. (1963)
COURTESY OF PORTSMOUTH CITY COUNCIL

Lillian's
10 Fratton Road
Telephone 23938
★ Permanent Waving Specialists   ★ Colouring   ★ Tinting   ★ Styling
★ Reasonable Prices

Lillian's
4 Walberant Buildings
Telephone 61615
PERSONAL SUPERVISION
BOTH SHOPS OPEN ALL DAY WEDNESDAY

The building, started after the war, continued in Hilsea. These flats, Loring House and Gerard House, with their very striking and distinctive design, were built in Conan Road in the late 1960s. (February 2002)

A Last Look at Rural and Military Life

The coronation was celebrated by a garden party in Hilsea Barracks which turned out to be the last big social event before the barracks closed. A 1953 close-up of some of the guests reveal the latest in 1950s' fashions.
COURTESY OF THE RLC MUSEUM

The long, full skirt, possibly made of taffeta, was the latest thing in 1953.
COURTESY OF THE RLC MUSEUM

The long skirt appears again, this time with pleats and stiletto heels. (1953) COURTESY OF THE RLC MUSEUM

A selection of fashionable hats in this 1953 shot. COURTESY OF THE RLC MUSEUM

These fox-fur stoles were all the rage in 1953 and usually had the fox's head hanging down at the front and his claws at the back. COURTESY OF THE RLC MUSEUM

A side view of the taffeta job, 1953.
COURTESY OF THE RLC MUSEUM

Tea, cucumber sandwiches and cakes on the lawn, 1953. COURTESY OF THE RLC MUSEUM

In polite society, ladies keep their gloves at the tea table, 1953.
COURTESY OF THE RLC MUSEUM

Soon to be demolished, the barracks were photographed in 1962 just before they disappeared. This is a shot of the main gate on the London Road. COURTESY OF J.A. HEWES

The sergeants' mess, 1962. This building still stands and is used by a local scout troop. COURTESY OF J.A. HEWES

St Barbara's was a very attractive garrison church, and the greatest loss of the site. It had been built in 1888 and in 1922, was dedicated to St Barbara, the patron saint of the RAOC and the Royal Artillery. It was made of corrugated iron which was common in late-Victorian times and often used for garrison churches. Inside, the walls were lined with boarding. It also housed a font, thought to be medieval, which had been dug up in the grounds of Gatcombe House. This photograph dates from 1928 and shows the entrance porch. There was also a Roman Catholic chapel near St Barbara's. It had originally been an army hut in Portsea and was moved to the Barracks after the First World War. It was also demolished. COURTESY OF RLC MUSEUM

A group photograph taken after the service to dedicate the altar rails in May 1931. COURTESY OF RLC MUSEUM

A 1953 view of the interior showing the wooden boarding on the walls and the traditional wooden pews.
COURTESY OF J.A. HEWES

A 1953 close-up of the altar and lovely stained glass windows. COURTESY OF J.A. HEWES

A postcard dating from the 1900s, showing the rear of the church and Hilsea pond, with the barracks in the background.
COURTESY OF JOHN BOWRING

Gatcombe House, 1962, the former officers' mess and the most elegant house in Hilsea. It is a three-storey, five-bay brick Georgian house built on a much older site. It became the officers' mess in 1877 and was altered and enlarged. There were many illustrious visitors to the officers' mess. The Duke of York came in 1922 before he married Elizabeth Boyes-Lyon, the late Queen Mother. Her Majesty Queen Elizabeth II came in 1958 accompanied by Prince Philip COURTESY OF J.A. HEWES

A very rare postcard, postmarked 23 December 1909, showing Hilsea Lodge, one of the houses of old rural Hilsea which was demolished and never replaced as the farmland was built over. Its name is retained in the modern building now situated next to Gatcombe House. COURTESY OF JOHN BOWRING

The Trolley Buses: 4 August 1934–27 July 1963

The trolley-bus wires criss-crossing at Hilsea roundabout were a familiar feature of the gateway to Portsmouth in the 1960s. The city was known for its complicated trolley-bus wire configurations and the place never looked quite the same once they had gone. COURTESY OF PORTSMOUTH CITY MUSEUM & RECORDS SERVICE

Hilsea roundabout photographed in the 1960s looking south towards the Copnor Road. The pedestrian bridge in the top of the picture crosses over the London Road from Military Road to the Portsmouth Grammar School playing fields. COURTESY OF PORTSMOUTH CITY MUSEUM & RECORDS SERVICE

There is much to see in this small 1967 picture, a last view of Portscreek before it was largely filled in during the construction of the motorway. This shot gives a good idea of its width and the fact that boats could navigate it. The lido is in the background and gives a last sight of the second set of entrance gates which were sited on the north side. They disappeared when the motorway was built. The diving tower is still there, too, but that was to go in 1971.
COURTESY OF J.A. HEWES

A 1960s' view of the London Road just before it was widened during construction of the new enlarged Portsbridge roundabout. Note the high chain-link fencing which separated the lido site from the road. COURTESY OF PORTSMOUTH CITY MUSEUM & RECORDS SERVICE

Probably the last aerial view of the gateway to Portsmouth with all the landmarks still intact – the lido entrance arch and tower, the Bastion Road House, the London Road and Portsbridge still in their 1920s' form. Most importantly, Portscreek was still a navigable stretch of water separating Portsea Island from the mainland. (1965)
COURTESY OF THE NEWS

The first to go. The Hilsea Lido entrance arch and tower is demolished and the end of the moat filled in on 13 December 1968 to make way for the widening of the London Road. COURTESY OF PORTSMOUTH CITY MUSEUM & RECORDS SERVICE

Another view, dated 13 December 1968, from the west side of London Road. The Christmas decorations in the window of the Bastion Road House garage make a sad contrast to the work of destruction about to begin. COURTESY OF PORTSMOUTH CITY MUSEUM & RECORDS SERVICE

Chapter 11 **1969–1999**

THE CONSTRUCTION OF THE M275 AND THE 1980s

The gateway to Portsmouth was about to undergo a dramatic alteration to its appearance. The 1970s and '80s gave Hilsea its modern-day look, with the construction of the motorway and the new Portsbridge roundabout. Modern housing and industrial estates were built on the sites of the old farms and former barracks. Not only had Hilsea now lost any military significance, but it was no longer the main route on to Portsea Island; in fact, it was to be by-passed altogether. The Hilsea Lines site had been scheduled as an Ancient Monument in 1964 and was finally acquired by the City Council in 1974 to begin a new life as a Conservation Area.

Hilsea Lido, too, began to go the way of the old fortifications, as it fell out of fashion and began to lose its original features. The diving tower followed the entrance arch and was demolished in 1971. Another favourite landmark to go was the Bastion Road House. One new building, however, was The News Centre which was constructed on empty ground next to the Southdown Bus Garage in the late 1960s, when The News transferred from its old Headquarters in Stanhope Road, Portsmouth.

One major effect of the massive land reclamation needed for the new motorway was to open up the gateway to Portsmouth in a way never imagined before. Instead of the rather intimate experience of entering Hilsea with its landmarks on a human scale, any driver entering Portsmouth now has the Hilsea Lines, the lido, the Stamshaw Esplanade and Tipner Lake exposed openly to their gaze as they negotiate the great curve of Tipner bridge. The civil engineer was to have the last word as water was turned into land.

An impressive 1969 aerial view of the massive project to widen the London Road, enlarge the Portsbridge roundabout and create the motorway from reclaimed land in Portsmouth Harbour. This view shows clearly just how much land was taken from the lido site and how much of Portscreek along the lido esplanade was filled in. This had the effect of ensuring that salt water could no longer be pumped from Portscreek for use in the swimming pools. Fresh water was pumped in from the mains supply but it was never the same.
COURTESY OF PORTSMOUTH CITY MUSEUM & RECORDS SERVICE

A photograph taken on 17 April 1969 looking west–east towards the dramatic view of the Highbury estate in Cosham.
COURTESY OF PORTSMOUTH CITY MUSEUM & RECORDS SERVICE

Another aerial view, from 1972, this time looking west, showing the completed Portsbridge roundabout in use, and the reclaimed land for the M275 which has almost crossed Tipner Lake. The distinctive shape of Hilsea Crescent shows up well and The News Centre can be seen in the bottom left-hand corner. The long, narrow buildings at the top left corner are a part of HMS *Phoenix*, a naval establishment which was also closed in the 1970s and housing built on the site. COURTESY OF PORTSMOUTH CITY MUSEUM & RECORDS SERVICE

The 1980s and More Changes

The children's playground in Alexandra Park has a new look and now we can see the motorway bridge in the far distance crossing Tipner Lake. A bus going over it is just visible. This photograph was taken by Ronald Lubbock (1905–98), a former City of Portsmouth Treasurer who took shots of familiar scenes around the city in the 1980s. His collection of over 1000 views forms an important part of Portsmouth's visual history. COURTESY OF PORTSMOUTH CITY COUNCIL

The children's playground was not to last much longer however, as the Mountbatten Centre was constructed on its site. It was officially opened by the Duke of York in 1983. This was to provide Portsmouth with a new indoor sports centre alongside the cycling and athletics track. By now, very little of the original Edwardian park remains but this shot, taken in January 2002, shows the old and the new – the original gates and the plaque commemorating the opening in 1907, with the new centre in the background.

A vista through the park, January 2002. A bandstand originally existed in the centre and the rustic shelter was more or less where the steps end today. The park must have made a wonderful sight back in 1907 with the band playing, the trees and flowers in full bloom and everyone in their Sunday-best Edwardian dress with flowery hats, of course, for the ladies. Not far away was the seashore so no doubt, there were a few sea breezes too! Alexandra Park was also the setting for the landing of Amy Johnson, the well-known pilot of the 1930s. She had flown down to Portsmouth for a civic reception and in the days before Portsmouth Airport was opened, the park was the next best thing.

THE BOOK OF HILSEA

A vista looking south–north along the London Road. This is another view by Ronald Lubbock which has hardly changed today. He just managed to capture Bradleys, the shop on the far left with the lovely Art Deco facade, before it was demolished and replaced by a block of flats in the 1990s. Date of photograph: 1980s.
COURTESY OF PORTSMOUTH CITY COUNCIL

A 1980s' view of the far west end of the moat overlooked by Tipner Lake and the motorway bridge, by Garrick Palmer. The steps up to the ramparts still remain but the trees have now disappeared.

A contemplative study of the reflection of the footbridge over the moat, by Garrick Palmer, 1986. This was demolished in 1999 after having been closed since 1995 and, at the time of writing, is due to be replaced. The toilets of the children's pool can be seen in the background as they looked before the doors and windows were blocked up.

A 1980s' study by Garrick Palmer where the gnarled tree trunks appear to echo the contorted angle of the footbridge over the London Road.

An atmospheric view along the moat, by Garrick Palmer, 1986. The tennis courts and former roller-skating rink were grassed over in the early 1990s but they are still visible in this shot.

Chapter 12 **1990–2002**

A NEW MILLENNIUM AND A GOLDEN JUBILEE

At the beginning of the twenty-first century, Hilsea's history comes over as something of a paradox. It is a place which was not part of Portsmouth but was entirely influenced by Portsmouth's development and the requirements of the military; did not belong to the mainland but was the nearest part of Portsea Island to it; never developed into a holiday resort but has the only lido in the area; a place defined by changing and contradictory military policies and landmarks long since gone.

Today, all these aspects stand together as a testament to the rich and varied history of 'the land raised in marsh' and the diverse communities who lived there, a history which is quite different from that of its surroundings yet which it owes entirely to its location as the gateway to Portsmouth.

The Barracks Site Today

Gatcombe House, always the most elegant building in Hilsea, as seen from its former gardens which are now run as a park by Portsmouth City Council. The house was extensively modernised and refurbished and reopened in 1986 by Lord Romsey as the head office of Warings Contractors Ltd. (November 2001)

The garden gates now look on to the Copnor Road and the former Civil Service Sports Ground. (November 2001)

The stylish rotunda in the far corner of the gardens has an unexpected history. It has no connection with Gatcombe House, being purchased by Portsmouth City Council from Crichel House in Dorset and erected in 1973. The Council took the view that as it was also of the eighteenth century, it would complement the house. The architect is unknown. (November 2001)

The 'Gospel Elm' plaque. This concrete base and its bronze plaque commemorated the site where John Wesley, the eighteenth-century preacher is believed to have preached. Originally, he stood under an elm tree and when the tree died a plaque was put in its place. This is the original memorial placed in 1909 being scrutinised by the late Lieutenant Colonel 'Frankie' Jones, date unknown.
COURTESY OF THE RLC MUSEUM

The bronze tablet was stolen and in 1972 this stone was put in its place. The wording is almost illegible on both memorials: 'Near this plaque stood a massive elm beneath which John Wesley preached during his ministry. This elm died eventually and in the centre of its shell the young elm now growing was planted by the following in the year 1909, the Reverend A.A.L. Gedge BA, Chaplain to the Forces, Hilsea: John Doe, Verger, Hilsea Garrison Church.' (November 2001)

A detail of the main gate with its original metal and brickwork. (November 2001)

The walls of the former barracks still stand alongside the London Road and the main gate still exists, too, although now leading to a housing estate as opposed to the guardroom. This view looks through the gate on to the London Road. (November 2001)

The former sergeants' mess is known as the Bert Mitchell Centre and is used by the local scout troop. Date of photograph: November 2001.

A study by Garrick Palmer of the other eighteenth-century building in Hilsea, a house opposite the former barracks on the west side of the London Road. This was probably used as officers' accommodation and has been considerably modernised and restored since. It is Grade II Listed. (February 2002)

On the last page of Cynthia Sherwood's impressive and comprehensive catalogue of memorials in Portsmouth, the stone plaque which replaced the Camp Cenotaph at Hilsea Barracks in 1948 is categorised as missing. In fact, it was taken down in 1972 and has been held in storage ever since by the City Museum. It has been unseen for thirty years and, at the time of writing, there are no plans to resite it. While remnants of the barracks site do remain, the one glaring omission is some sort of memorial to all the men who served there. Nowadays, when barracks sites are sold off for housing, developers are more sympathetic to the idea of providing a memorial within the costs of the development, but this was not the case in the 1970s. (February 2002) COURTESY OF PORTSMOUTH CITY MUSEUM & RECORDS SERVICE

Gatcombe Park Primary School now occupies part of the barracks site. The name, The Ridings, commemorates the riding school that existed here.
(February 2002)

Hilsea Lido's 60th Anniversary

Hilsea Lido celebrated the 60th anniversary of its official opening on 24 July 1995. An exhibition to commemorate the anniversary was held in the Norrish Central Library from 24 July to 12 August 1995. This poster was designed in July 1995 especially for the exhibition by Rex Hawkesworth ARIBA.

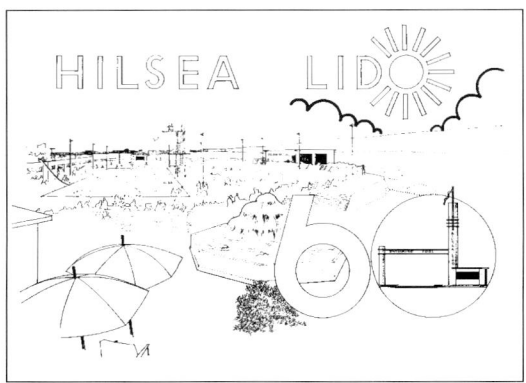

The late Esther Mullinger is shown here with me on the opening day of the exhibition on 24 July 1995. Esther was present at the opening in 1935, and here she is sixty years later to the day, at the exhibition to commemorate it! COURTESY OF ALLAN SMITH

The great weight of water that is Tipner Lake at high tide looms over the lido and the moat almost threatening to engulf it. The sea wall, a very clever piece of civil engineering, is just sufficient to contain it and cradles the lido buildings effortlessly. The interplay between the three water levels is a great feature of this area; the high-tide level of Tipner Lake, the lower level of the moat and the lower level still of the swimming pool. (1993)

A chance to see the main pool almost empty. The design of it shows up very well with its rectangular 'shallow ends' and diving pit in the centre which is 15ft deep. The diving tower was situated in the centre of the site where the railings are now. The bathers' refreshment stand at the far west end was demolished early in 1995. The steps at the edge were originally the steps up to the children's water chute and these were also demolished. (1993)

The children's paddling pool is as popular as it ever was in this shot taken 26 August 2001, but the cascade disappeared in the 1960s.

A play area was added to the site in 1995. (August 2001)

These humble toilets situated on the edge of the lido site were among the original buildings when the area was landscaped into a pleasure park in the early 1930s. They were demolished in 1998 and a modern building put in their place. (1998)

The rear aspect of the toilets, facing the lido site. (1998)

One Bridge, Two Columns and Three Plaques

A close-up of the west face of the modern Portsbridge showing the tunnel leading to the centre of the roundabout – quite unnavigable for boats these days! A century on and children are again sitting on the stonework, perhaps because the main pool of the lido was closed during the summer season of 2001 for the first time since the Second World War. (August 2001)

A view from the east showing the two lamp columns remaining on this side. (November 2001)

The plaque on the west face of the bridge commemorating the reconstruction of Portsbridge in 1927. (February 2002)

The plaque commemorating the reopening of Portscreek to navigation between Portsmouth and Langstone Harbours. Portscreek had been closed from 1939–1945 by a wartime emergency bridge known as the 'Pipe' bridge. This had been done in case Portsbridge was damaged by bombing and was near the spot where the Peronne Road bridge is today. This plaque also commemorates the role played by the small boats which left these shores to rescue the British troops from Dunkirk in 1940. (February 2002)

The third plaque commemorates the opening of the South Coast Trunk Road and Farlington and Cosham Bypass in 1970. (February 2002)

A Landmark Lost

The United Services Garage in the London Road was demolished in 1997 and replaced by a modern garage in spite of local protests. It had originally been a coach station and the headquarters for Solent Coaches. (1997)

The 1930s-style clock was retrieved, however, and rehung in the City of Portsmouth Preserved Transport Depot in Broad Street, Old Portsmouth. It had been installed in 1946 and was a vital aid to the workers at the garage as many of them did not possess wrist-watches in those days. (October 2001)

A New Playground

A new children's playground, now a play area, was opened in Alexandra Park in 1995 – its fourth manifestation and situated by the main gate. Gone, however, are the dangerous things that go round and round or up and down and in their place, static climbing frames and miniature slides. The swings, at least, are the only items to be more or less unchanged in half a century. (January 2002)

The cycle track at Alexandra Park is still very popular. Here, cyclists at the pavilion prepare for a run. (February 2002)

Sunday morning is football time at the North End Recreation Ground. (February 2002)

The Gateway Today

This 1980s' aerial view looking west–east shows the Portsbridge roundabout as it is today. The Southdown Bus Garage, now the Co-op Depot still stands, shown in the right-hand corner, the lido site is shown on the left, the site of the prefabs, now Lynx House, is seen in the top left-hand corner. The footbridge over the moat was demolished in 1999 and, at the time of writing, is due to be replaced. COURTESY OF RON DOOLER

A study by Garrick Palmer, taken in February 2002, of the old Portsbridge looking east, with the motorway on the left. Before the roundabout was widened, this was the road into Portsmouth. Now it is a car park

A clearer view of the old A3 and Portsbridge, by Garrick Palmer, January 2002. Gone are the long, clear vistas of the 1950s across to Cosham and Portsdown Hill, and the pleasant walks over Portsbridge. Nowadays, pedestrians have to find their way down uninviting underpasses while traffic hurtles overhead.

A view of the approach to the Portsbridge roundabout, by Garrick Palmer, January 2002. The motorway bridge forms a new type of fortification over the gateway to Portsmouth!

The London Road looking south, by Garrick Palmer, January 2002. No trolley-bus wires these days but three lanes of traffic leading to the centre of Portsmouth. The London Road originally reached across to the bottom right-hand corner of the picture with the lido entrance arch and tower slightly further along out of the picture. Now, all this area is a lay-by for buses and cars.

The second shaft looking north. The building on the right is still part of the group of Portsmouth Water buildings. Roebuck House can be seen in the far distance. (November 2001)

Once over Portsbridge, it is still possible to see the entrance to the shafts of the tunnels for the water supply although the cages over the top of them were removed in the 1970s. (November 2001)

Lynx House, the modern building now replacing the prefabs. (November 2001)

The Portsmouth Water Company building shown just before its demolition in 1999 having lasted seventy years.

A McDonalds stands on the site in spite of vociferous local protests. (November 2001)

In spite of the motorway, the Cosham Bowling Green and the Highbury Buildings shopping parade in the background, built in 1935, are remarkably unchanged. Owing to the rerouting of the A3, they are now a backwater and not the landmarks along the way into Portsmouth that they once were. (November 2001)

A Few More Changes

A vista looking south past the The News Centre. In the right-hand corner are Hilsea Market and the new garage which replaced the United Services Garage. (February 2002)

A quick glance at the London Road shows that the First Church of Christ, Scientist is still there and looking very much the same apart from a few minor alterations. (November 2001)

The reading room is almost unchanged but the bus shelter and the National Westminster Bank look rather different from the 1950s! (November 2001)

This postcard is postmarked 29 July 1907 and shows the Hilsea Obelisk as it was in the early 1900s. The Green Posts pub looks much the same today.
COURTESY OF JOHN BOWRING

The same vista today, taken February 2002. Apart from the modern flats and the cars, old Hilsea and the London Road are remarkably unchanged.

A vista looking north, by Garrick Palmer, January 2002.

The Hilsea Lines

Today, the appearance of the northern border of Hilsea is a testament to the work of the engineer, both civil and military. The Hilsea Lines stretch for 2.5km along the north shore of Portsea Island and cover an area of over 80 hectares. They were constructed one hundred and fifty years ago by armies of military labourers and still stand, now managed by Portsmouth City Council both as a Scheduled Ancient Monument and a Conservation Area. The outline of the bastions and walls, known as curtains, shows up very clearly here. Alongside, runs the motorway, constructed by civil engineers.

The bridge across the motorway used as a footbridge runs from Peronne Road in Hilsea to Tudor Crescent in Cosham. It is believed to be the site of the original crossing at Portsbridge used by the Tudors. Henry VIII is thought to have constructed a fortification there and the name Tudor Crescent reflects this association. The military connection remains too, as the 1930s' building underneath the bridge's curve is used by Cosham Territorial Army Training Centre, HQ 'B' Company, Hampshire and the Isle of Wight Army Cadet Force. (1980s)
COURTESY OF RON DOOLER

Bastion 3. (1980s)
COURTESY OF RON DOOLER

THE BOOK OF HILSEA

Bastion 5. (1980s)
COURTESY OF RON DOOLER

The Sally Port entrance to Scott Road. (1980s) COURTESY OF RON DOOLER

A gun emplacement. There is one at the rear of each bastion and they are now surrounded by woodland. (1980s)
COURTESY OF RON DOOLER

This shot shows local schoolchildren in 1997, taking part in a replanting scheme on the land between the moat and the motorway on the east side of the London Road. A thousand trees were planted by 400 schoolchildren to provide screening for the motorway.
COURTESY OF RON DOOLER

More planting. (1997)
COURTESY OF RON DOOLER

A group from the British Trust for Conservation Volunteers who came down to help.
COURTESY OF RON DOOLER

Children feeding the ducks, taken on the railway footbridge underneath the railway line on the far eastern borders of Hilsea. (1997)
COURTESY OF RON DOOLER

A train passing through. (1997)
COURTESY OF RON DOOLER

The Conservation Area supports a variety of wildlife. Here, a heron is seen at the far east end of Portscreek. (1997)
COURTESY OF RON DOOLER

Portcreek 1917, by Wilfred Appleby

Ebb-Tide has drained the creek. A lonely shag
deplores the dreary scene; while clouds,
too weak to rain, exude a humid mist. The bleak
long creek becomes a trough of miry quag.

The skylark shivers in her dew-chilled nest;
Thro' dimness crawls a sad, black lazy train
crossing the bridge with requiem refrain;
even the tangled grasses lie depressed.

A shimmering in the east – . A fanning breeze
dispels the dismal pall that veiled the sun.
A full tide flows, the lark song has begun
and emerald lizards bask in warmth and ease.

Hail to the sun: The greatful Earth rejoices
and sings her Gloria with many voices.

A Favourite Walk

The presence of the motorway, with its continual movement and traffic noise, has not quite managed to rob Tipner Lake of its air of wild remoteness. The walk around the esplanade from Hilsea Lido to Alexandra Park is as popular as it always was. There is still the tang of the sea on the breeze, the seagulls resting on the mudflats, the geese feeding at the shoreline and interesting things to find among the shingle when the tide is out; no small boats these days, though. (February 2002)

The motorway bridge frames Portchester Castle in the distance and the newly erected masts are just visible in daylight. No one crosses to Horsea Island by the old wadeway now although Horsea Lane still exists with its path past the allotments down to the old shoreline, and the ramp can still be seen near the start of the wadeway. A footbridge is marked on one map leading from HMS *Phoenix* over to Horsea Island but this disappeared after the war. Today, only cars go where once small boats and fishermen went. (February 2002)

154

A New Millennium and a New Landmark

The Sails of the South. This is the first new landmark at the gateway to Portsmouth since the construction of the motorway. A Trimast sculpture, erected in 2001 by Headley Greentree and the Portsmouth and Southeast Hampshire Partnership, marks the new millennium. Date of photograph: September 2001.

A Golden Jubilee

In the year of the Golden Jubilee of Queen Elizabeth II, who better to have the last word on Hilsea than the people from the oldest surviving community, Hilsea Crescent, now over seventy years old? Many of the children shown in the photographs of the 1940s' coach-outing and the coronation street party remained, as adults, either living in Hilsea or very close to their roots. The Hilsea 1940s' Club was formed in 1999 and this picture shows the members at their first reunion on 14 July 1999 which was held at the Northern Parade Community Centre. The organisers, Bill Ferrett and Ron Boyland are shown kneeling, first and second from the left.

Many of the ladies shown here are members of the original families who moved into Hilsea at the end of the 1920s. The Thursday Club meets every week in the Fred Gent Memorial Hall, for bingo and other social activities. The club is soon to celebrate its 20th anniversary as it was founded in 1982 by Elsie Craigie, fifth down on the right side. It has been run for the last five years by Pat Cornish, sixth down on the right side.

Elsie has lived in Hilsea for seventy-two years, in the same house, and brought up four sons there. She has memories of Northern Parade when it was still open land, the Oakwood pub and St Francis' Church were the Hogshead Pond, and the nearest shops to Hilsea Crescent were either in Cosham or Stamshaw. The community was very close and tightly knit, known for its large families, neighbourliness and longevity, particularly of the ladies!

Lilian Dugan, seen first left, and her sister Hilda, right foreground, were two of 15 children who came to Hilsea as a family in 1928. Their mother lost two children but 13 survived and 11 are still alive today. The oldest sister is 86 and the youngest 62.

Daisy Barton (née Collier), shown second left, celebrated her eighth birthday in Hilsea in 1928. She has lived in the same house for fifty-two years where she also brought up four children.

Joyce Arnett, shown ninth down on the right, has lived in Hilsea since 1927. She celebrated her 80th birthday at the meeting on the day the photograph was taken, 7 February 2002. Like Esther Mullinger, she was present at the official opening of Hilsea Lido in 1935 and her photograph appeared in *The News* half a century later on 26 July 1985 at the main pool when the lido celebrated its 50th anniversary.

Other well-known Hilsea families were the Morgans with 12 children and the Smallbones with ten. There were some even larger families, with 13 or more children, who were rehoused elsewhere. The houses had three good-sized bedrooms but the children had to sleep top to bottom in the bed, the boys in one, the girls in another and the baby in with mum!

The creation of the Hilsea Lido pleasure park not long after their arrival was considered to be a godsend for all the community with the children spending as much time there as they could. While many children did move away from Hilsea, many remained. The houses and gardens have hardly changed in seventy years and the area is still a most popular and pleasant place in which to live.

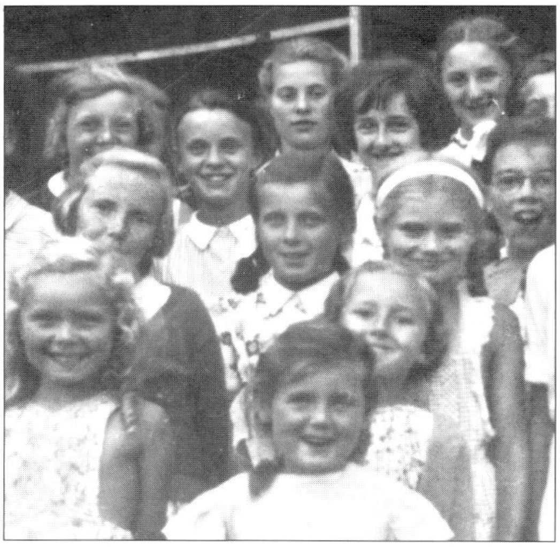

BIBLIOGRAPHY

Primary Sources

Childers, Colonel Spencer, CB, RE, Editor. *A Mariner of England: An Account of the Career of William Richardson from Cabin Boy in the Merchant Service to Warrant Officer in the Royal Navy (1780–1819) as Told by Himself*, Conway Maritime Press: 1st edition 1908, New Impression 1970.

City of Portsmouth. *Tenants' Handbook: Leigh Park Edition*, The British Publishing Company Limited, 1963.
Souvenir Programme of the Coronation Celebrations, Portsmouth 1953.
Portsmouth and Southsea Official Guide, various years, 1934–2001.

Guide to Southsea and Portsmouth with the Neighbouring District, second edition, Ward Lock & Co. London, about 1930s.

The News, Portsmouth, various issues, 1930–2002.
Brown, Ron. Nostalgia/The Way We Were, *The News*, Portsmouth, various articles, 1980–2002.

Secondary Sources

Bardell, Mark. *Portsmouth: History and Guide*, Tempus Publishing Limited, 2001.

Coates, Richard. *The Place-Names of Hampshire*, B.T. Batsford Limited, London, 1989.

Cox, Barry. *Portsmouth Trolley Buses*, Middleton Press, 2001.

Cranfield, Ingrid. *Art Deco House Style: An Architectural and Interior Design Source Book*, David & Charles, 2001.

Drummond, Maldwin & McInnes, Robin, Editors. *The Book of the Solent Including the Isle of Wight Coastal Voyage*, Cross Publishing, Chale, Isle of Wight, 2001.

Eyles, Allen. *Old Cinemas: A Shire Book*, Shire Publications Ltd, 2001.

Gates, William G. *Portsmouth in the Past*, first published Portsmouth 1926, republished S.R. Publishers Ltd, 1972.

Hampshire Telegraph & Post. *Pictorial Souvenir 1799–1949*, Portsmouth & Sunderland Newspapers Ltd, London, about 1949.

Howell, Alexander N.Y., Compiler. *Notes on the Topography of Portsmouth Together With Historical and Statistical Information*, W.H. Barrell Limited, Portsmouth, 1913.

Lloyd, David W. *The Buildings of Portsmouth and Its Environs*, Portsmouth City Council, 1974.

Memories of Portsmouth. True North Books Limited, 1999.

More Memories of Portsmouth, 2001.

Mitchell, Gary. *Hilsea Lines and Portsbridge*, Solent Papers No. 4, G.H. Mitchell, 1988.

Moignard, David. *North End: The History*, JR Printers, Portsmouth, about 2000.
Nash, Andy. 'A.E. Cogswell: Architect Within a Victorian City, the School of Architecture', unpublished dissertation, Portsmouth Polytechnic, 1975.

Offord, John. *Churches, Chapels and Places of Worship on Portsea Island*, John Harman, Southsea, 1989.

Pevsner, Nikolaus & Lloyd, David. *The Buildings of England: Hampshire and the Isle of Wight*, Penguin Books, 1990.

Portsmouth City Council, *The Portsmouth Papers*, various authors, 1967–2000.
    Public Monuments and Memorials in the City of Portsmouth or Otherwise in the Ownership of The Corporation, 1972.
    City and Ward Profiles, 1998.
    An Everyday Atlas of Portsmouth, 1991.
    Hilsea Lines Management Plan, Third Revision, 1998.

Portsmouth Museums and Records Service. *Portsmouth in the Twentieth Century: A Photographic History*, Halsgrove, 1999.

Quail, Sarah. *The Origins of Portsmouth and the First Charter*, Portsmouth Paper No. 65, Portsmouth City Council, 1994.

Quail, Sarah & Stedman, J. *Images of Portsmouth*, The Breedon Books Publishing Company, Derby, 1993.

Queen's Harbour Master, Portsmouth. *A Small Craft Guide to Portsmouth Harbour and its Approaches*, The Crown Estate, no date.

Riley, Ray. *Railways and Portsmouth Society 1847–1947*, Portsmouth Paper No. 70, Portsmouth City Council, 2000.

Rogers, Peter N. *Cosham With Widley and Hilsea in Old Picture Postcards*, European Library/Zaltbommer Netherlands, 1986.

Rogers, Peter N. & Francis David F. *Portsmouth in Old Photographs*, Alan Sutton, 1989.
    Portsmouth in Old Picture Postcards, European Library/Zaltbommer Netherlands, 1986.

Powell, Michael. *Spithead: The Navy's Anvil*, Redan & Vedette (Agencies) Ltd., 1977.

Sadden, John. *Portsmouth: In Defence of the Realm*, Phillimore, 2001.

Salvetti, Geoffrey. *The Hilsea Lines*, Portsmouth Grammar School Monograph 6, 2001.

Shemeld, Gilbert. *Portsmouth: A Description By Contemporary Eye-Witnesses 1540–1973*: Selected and Edited by Gilbert Shemeld, Topographical Series No. 1, E.J. Burnett, Portsmouth, 1973.

Sherwood, Cynthia. *Monuments of Portsmouth*, unpublished catalogue, about 1991.

Smith, Jane. 'The Discovery of Hilsea Lido: An Exploratory Case Study in Urban History', unpublished dissertation, Southampton Institute, 1996.

Stark, Harry Leonard. 'James Carsley, His Story: Compiled by a Great-great-grandson', unpublished family history, Mitcham, 1979.

Wills, Victoria. 'Modern Movement Houses in Hampshire and Sussex, 1927–1939', unpublished dissertation, Portsmouth Polytechnic, 1985.

Worker's Educational Association. 'Memories From Over the Lines', 1995.

'Yesterday', various, numbers 1–32, *The News*, 1988–1990.

While every effort has been made to trace all the copyright holders, we apologise to any unacknowledged copyright holders and would like to hear from them.